Southampton's Railways

Bert Moody

TRANSPORT
Atlantic
PUBLISHERS

As a result of major engineering works being carried out on the main line during 1965/6 in connection with electrification, various diversions were made at weekends. Here is West Country class No. 34046 *Braunton* with the 'Bournemouth Belle' passing through Woolston.
D. Walden

Contents

Atlantic Publishers, Trevithick House, West End, Penryn, Cornwall TR10 8HE

ISBN: 0 906899 78 8   © Bert Moody, 1992

Printed by The Amadeus Press Ltd, Huddersfield, West Yorkshire
First published 1992 by Waterfront Publications. This edition 1997.

Introduction

About forty years ago when employed in the District Traffic Superintendent's office at Southampton Central my interest in railway history was given a great impetus by the enthusiasm shown for the subject by the late Mr C.N. Anderson, who was the Assistant District Traffic Superintendent at Southampton for twenty years and had taken a special interest in the railway history of the area.

During my railway career I found that I was often in the right place at the right time when records were being disposed of or transferred to other departments, and so discovered items of information not recorded elsewhere, resulting in my having collected a considerable amount of information relating to railways in the Southampton area.

From time to time when giving talks on the subject, people have suggested that the information should be collated into a book. Like many similar works of this nature there are still certain local aspects which have not been completely resolved and as time goes by are less likely to be. However, when reading this book I hope that it will give to others some small part of the enjoyment and pleasure which I have gained over the years through my interest in the railways of Southampton.

I have received a great deal of help from my many friends – to them all my very grateful thanks. I am most indebted for the help given by Malcolm Snellgrove who from time to time manages to succeed in finding the final elusive piece of information to complete a story. I would like to thank the following for their help in various ways: John A. Bailey, Desmond Cull, Dennis Cullum, Ted Fry, Geoffrey Gardiner, John B. Horne, Tony Sedgwick, Will Stearn and Peter Swift. The staff at Southampton Reference Library and at Southampton Maritime Museum have given considerable help and also Roger Hardingham of Waterfront Publications. Finally, a special thanks to Alma, my wife, for her help and support for my many interests during the whole of our married life.

Southampton Railways – As It Could Have Been

During the last century Southampton with its excellent potential including the developing docks was often the king–pin of several schemes for proposed railways in the south of England, in addition the Great Western Railway for many years were most anxious to get a foothold in Southampton , and in this respect they were often given much local support by people who wished to break the monopoly held by the LSWR. How different the railway scene in Southampton would have been if only one or two of these proposals had materialised.

If the Southampton Harbour Commissioners in the 1840s had taken kindly to the use of steam engines the lines connecting the LSWR with the Southampton & Dorchester Railway could well have been via the waterfront instead of through the tunnel under the town. In 1846 the Manchester & Southampton Railway being an extension of the Midland Railway from Cheltenham was proposed and only very narrowly failed to pass through Parliament.

There was a proposal in 1860 to build a Petersfield – Bishops Waltham – Botley railway and in the following year a Southampton extension was proposed to pass via South Stoneham to a station on the west side of town, but this failed to pass the Parliamentary committee. Also in 1861 a scheme for a short Shirley Railway was considered. This line would have left the Royal Pier and after crossing the LSWR near the West station, it would have passed northwards along the eastern side of Hill Lane, then along the line of Wilton Road to the Dale Valley area and on to Nursling where a junction with the Andover & Redbridge Railway was proposed.

One major scheme which nearly reached fruition and would have had a great effect on the town was the Didcot, Newbury & Southampton Railway which planned in 1882 to extend from Winchester Cheesehill station to Southampton with stations at Chilworth, Shirley and at the west end of Bargate Street on land to be reclaimed, now part of the site at present occupied by Pirelli General Cable Works.

The line would have passed under Winchester Road and the station at Shirley would have been in the vicinity of the recreation ground in St. James Road. In fact there are still three roads in that area having links with the scheme – Newbury Road and Didcot Road, while the third – Stratton Road – was known as Station Road until 1903. The line would have crossed the LSWR on a bridge between Southampton West station and the Tunnel mouth. In fact construction of the embankment and the arches for the bridge was commenced on land between the Polygon and Hill Lane. Owing to a shortage of money the work was stopped and subsequently abandoned. Agreement was made with the LSWR for the connection to be made at Shawford Junction. which was brought into use on 4th September 1891. The remains of part of the embankment off Hill Lane could, however, be seen for many years.

Another scheme which would have had considerable effect on the local scene was one put forward by the LSWR. Prior to the First World War plans were drawn up for the construction of additional docks including a large drydock on the Woolston side of the River Itchen. In 1909 the Railway Company acquired a considerable area of land and the foreshore and these docks would have been rail served for it was the intention to provide a connection with the St. Denys – Fareham line about half a mile the Netley side of Sholing station – the connection facing for trains from Southampton. In conjunction with the scheme consideration was given to providing an additional spur at St. Denys to enable trains to run direct from the Netley Line to Eastleigh and on to Basingstoke and London, thus a triangle would have been provided at St. Denys. With the outbreak of war in 1914 the plans were put into cold storage and on the termination of hostilities plans were developed for the Docks extension to be provided between Southampton and Millbrook – the site of the Western Docks of today.

There is no doubt that the local railway scene could have been a lot different.

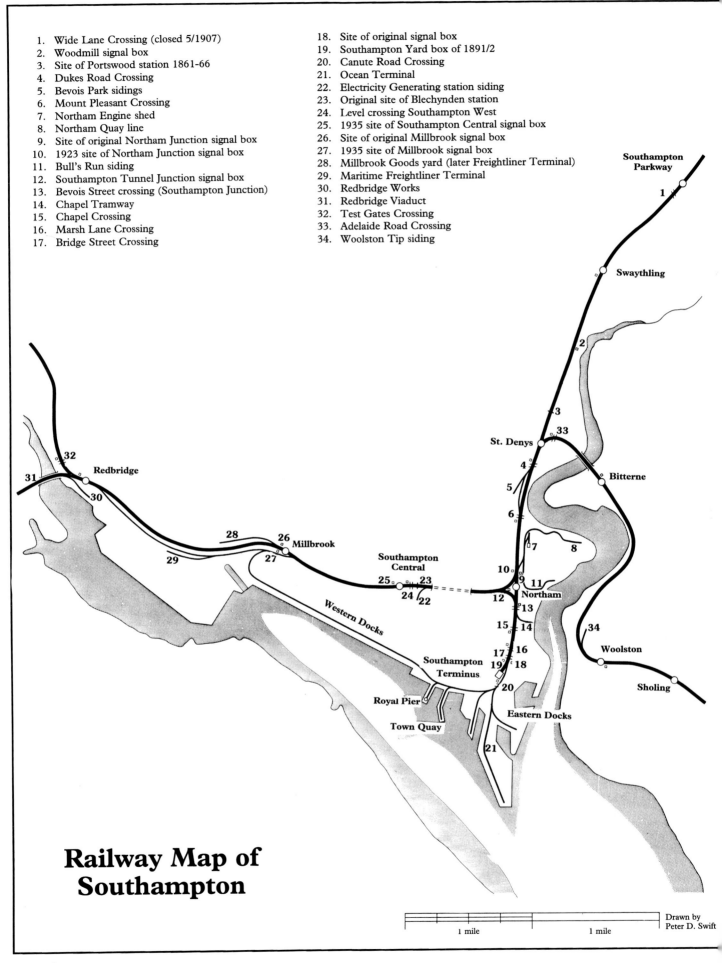

1. Wide Lane Crossing (closed 5/1907)
2. Woodmill signal box
3. Site of Portswood station 1861-66
4. Dukes Road Crossing
5. Bevois Park sidings
6. Mount Pleasant Crossing
7. Northam Engine shed
8. Northam Quay line
9. Site of original Northam Junction signal box
10. 1923 site of Northam Junction signal box
11. Bull's Run siding
12. Southampton Tunnel Junction signal box
13. Bevois Street crossing (Southampton Junction)
14. Chapel Tramway
15. Chapel Crossing
16. Marsh Lane Crossing
17. Bridge Street Crossing
18. Site of original signal box
19. Southampton Yard box of 1891/2
20. Canute Road Crossing
21. Ocean Terminal
22. Electricity Generating station siding
23. Original site of Blechynden station
24. Level crossing Southampton West
25. 1935 site of Southampton Central signal box
26. Site of original Millbrook signal box
27. 1935 site of Millbrook signal box
28. Millbrook Goods yard (later Freightliner Terminal)
29. Maritime Freightliner Terminal
30. Redbridge Works
31. Redbridge Viaduct
32. Test Gates Crossing
33. Adelaide Road Crossing
34. Woolston Tip siding

Southampton Parkway

Swaythling

St. Denys

Bitterne

Woolston

Sholing

Redbridge

Millbrook

Southampton Central

Western Docks

Northam

Southampton Terminus

Royal Pier

Town Quay

Eastern Docks

Railway Map of Southampton

Drawn by
Peter D. Swift

1 mile   1 mile

Early Developments

In 1825 a suggestion was made for the formation of a London, Portsmouth & Southampton railway, but this was never developed, and the first real moves to provide a railway between London and Southampton were made following a meeting, which was held on 6th October 1830 at Bugle Hall, the home of Mr. A.R. Dottin, M.P. for Southampton. As a result of this meeting a prospectus was issued in respect of the Southampton, London and Branch Railway Company. The Branch which was to run from Basingstoke to Bath and Bristol was never built.

Initially no great interest was created locally for the scheme, it being argued by some that Southampton was not important enough to have such rapid communication, and some of the inhabitants regarded it as rather a mad enterprise. However, further meetings were held, and at one in Southampton on 26th February 1831 the formation of the Southampton, London and Branch Railway and Dock Company was agreed. Following a further meeting in London on 23rd January 1832, the prospectus for the proposed railway was published, showing the capital as £1,000,000 in £50 shares. The projected docks and the branch were both omitted – it being left for the docks to be developed by a separate company.

The railway became known as the London & Southampton, and on the 25th July 1834, the Royal Assent was given to the Bill for making a railway – "commencing at the River Thames, at or near Nine Elms in the parish of Battersea in the county of Surrey, to the shore or beach at or near a place called the Marsh in the parish of Saint Mary in the town and county town of Southampton".

The original capital authorised did not prove sufficient and it was necessary to obtain a second Act, which was passed on 30th June 1837, authorising an additional £400,000 with loans up to £130,000.

The construction of the railway took place at a somewhat leisurely pace. In the Southampton area the foreshore from Dukes Road to Mount Pleasant extended to what became Empress Road, and it was necessary for the line from just south of Portswood to Mount Pleasant to be constructed on an embankment with several arches. The line from Nine Elms to Basingstoke was opened on 10th June 1839. On the same day the portion of line between Winchester and Northam was also brought into use, stage coaches being used between Basingstoke and Winchester to link the two portions of railway. The eventual terminus of the line on the Marsh in Southampton was not completed and a temporary station was provided at Northam on the north side of New Road/Northam Road. In addition the Railway Company was in dispute with the Northam Bridge Company concerning the level crossing which had been constructed at Northam Road.

Just prior to the opening of the railway the *Hampshire Independent* of the 1st June 1839 reported that an engine of 16 horse power, built by the firm of Summers, Groves & Day, who were shipbuilders and owned the Iron Foundry, Mill Place, Millbrook had been placed on the line for trials.

An Eastleigh to Dorchester train just south of Swaythling hauled by an unidentified Adams Jubilee class locomotive about 1896/7.
E.W. Fry collection

Canute Road Crossing – On 16th August 1902 the Coronation Naval Review for King Edward VII took place, and here we have engine No. 714, one of Drummond's 'T9s' hauling a special train with passengers for the Review across Canute Road into the Docks via No. 3 Dock Gate. The picture shows so much of interest – the man in the middle of the road protecting the movement of the train with his red flag and bell, a practice which continued right up until October 1981, when the existing flashing lights were installed. To the left of the engine the line giving access to the Town Quay and Royal Pier can be clearly seen and the line just outside the Dock Gate and passing over the track on which the train is travelling also led to the Town Quay and gave access to the LSWR system through the sidings shown in the background. In the centre of the roadway are the tram lines leading to the Floating Bridge which the Corporation agreed to remove when the road bridge at St. Denys Dukes Road was completed. Another interesting feature is the large cab yard which existed on the Canute Road side of the LSWR terminus. This was altered when the extensions to the South Western Hotel were carried out in the 1920s.

Author's collection

The Opening Day

The first train was scheduled to start at half past seven o'clock in the morning of the 10th June 1839 from Northam, and well before that time the vicinity of the station and the lineside was crowded with spectators. The stage coach from the Royal Hotel was, however, delayed and the train did not start until nearly eight o'clock. The *Hampshire Advertiser* of the 15th June 1839 reported that .... "the engine named *Pegasus* – a very powerful engine, beautifully made, and glittering in a profusion of brasswork; her tender and Engineer were placed in front, four carriages holding – the best eighteen, and the second class from twenty four to thirty passengers each, were attached, the stage coach was placed on its truck, some attendant policemen and porters found seats outside and sundry workmen in an extra drag. Presently, a hiss was made by *Pegasus* – clouds of smoke issued from its netted mouth – showers of fire fell on the road beneath, it began to move, slowly at first, as if feeling its way – then quick – quicker – the shrill rumbling sound of metal drums was heard, and the delighted passengers found themselves speeding along at a rate of more than thirty miles an hour".

The same paper contained a detailed account of the carriages – "travelling inside a first class coach is equal in every respect to travelling by a well appointed coach on the common roads. The seat being divided into three, with arm rests on each side of each person, preventing any overcrowding, and the windows can be opened or closed, no inconvenience need be sustained. The second class carriages being open, are only comfortable for those who sit with their back to the engine, those facing it compels an incessant application of the handkerchief to the eyes from the fine dust which is always blowing in."

The first journey of twelve miles to Winchester was accomplished in twenty six minutes, the second in twenty four minutes and the return journeys in twenty and twenty one minutes respectively. During the whole day *Pegasus* continued to haul trains, generally of six carriages, well filled with passengers between Northam and Winchester.

In June 1839 the London & Southampton Railway obtained powers to construct a line from Bishopstoke (now Eastleigh) to Gosport, and under the same Act the name of the Company was changed to the London & South Western Railway in order to cover the wider aspects of the railway.

On the 15th July 1839 the *Hampshire Chronicle* reported that the building at the terminus on the Marsh was nearly completed, and by the end of that month trains would start from the terminus. In September, however, a meeting of the directors decided that the terminus would not be brought into use until the whole line from Nine Elms was completed so the temporary station at Northam remained in use for the service to and from Winchester.

In August 1839 Summers, Groves & Day produced a second locomotive – a six wheeled version named *Southampton*.

An engraving made of the LSWR terminus in March 1841. Whether the engraver made a mistake or whether alterations were made to the building very early in its life is not known, but all other available pictures of the building show the upper windows much larger. The building remains today in use as The Stanley Casino. The building with the white flag, approximately on the site of Union Castle house today is marked 'Southampton Dock House'. *Author's collection*

The line throughout between Nine Elms and Southampton was brought into use on 11th May 1840, and although the usual flags and bunting were displayed on various buildings, there were no formal celebrations in the town on the day to mark the event. The first train left the terminus at half past six, hauled by the engine *Mars*, but failed by bursting of one of the tubes on the engine at Andover Road (renamed Micheldelver in 1856), and then suffered the ignominy of being drawn by horses to Basingstoke – the horses must have found it hard going particularly through the tunnels!

The first class train consisting of five first class carriages left at ten o'clock. Some of the directors of the Railway Company left Nine Elms at 8.00 a.m. in a train of thirteen first class carriages, hauled by the engine *Venus*, and arrived at the terminus at 11.30 a.m.

The dispute with the Northam Bridge Company centred on the question as to whether the Bridge Company's road over which the railway company had laid their tracks on the level, was a turnpike road – if it was, a bridge had to be provided. Initially judgement was given that the road was not a turnpike road, but this was subsequently reversed, when the Bridge Company appealed. By the end of May 1840 it was reported that the construction of the bridge was well underway, so the level crossing only remained in use for a few months after the complete opening of the line.

Southampton West station, formerly Blechynden, as seen from the top of the tunnel. The yard on the 'up' side was extremely small and the station platforms were quite short. In the background the water can be seen coming up nearly to the edge of the railway formation as the line disappears round the corner towards Millbrook.

Cope collection

Originally there was only one station in the Southampton area, which much later was given the title of Southampton Terminus. This impressive station building, which was designed by Sir William Tite, cost £10,500. The original station building remains today, now in use as a casino, but the majority of the later additions were demolished during 1984/5. Initially only two platforms were provided, one for arrivals and the other for departures.

The fares from London to Southampton in 1840 were first class – £1.00; on mixed trains it was 18s/– (90 pence) first class and 12s/– (60 pence) second class. Third class cost 7s/– (35 pence) and they travelled by goods train, mainly in uncovered wagons. A local paper quoted that at times the third class passengers, on arrival at their destinations, looked more like black and white minstrels!

The first class trains, of which there were two a day, covered the journey in three hours, while the Goods trains took about six hours.

The formation of the Southampton Dock Company was authorised by an Act of Parliament in May 1836, the foundation stone being laid on 12th October 1838, and the dock, later known as the Outer Dock (the Ocean Village of today) was brought into use in August 1842, and the railway was extended across Canute Road to serve that dock.

Developments Westwards

In 1844, Charles Castleman, a solicitor of Ringwood and Wimborne, put forward a scheme to provide a railway from Southampton to Dorchester. After various meetings it was decided that the Southampton & Dorchester Railway would pass via Brockenhurst, Ringwood, Wimborne, Poole and Wareham. Included in the proposals was the provision of a new station near the Royal Pier at Southampton, which would have involved a line being provided along the waterfront from Millbrook. From this proposed new station it was the intention that a tramway would be constructed to the LSWR terminus, thus linking the two systems and making through workings possible. The alternative scheme for a connection between the LSWR and the Southampton & Dorchester was by means of a tunnel under the town with a junction being made just north of the LSWR terminus.

Southampton Corporation and many townspeople were in favour of the waterfront line as it was felt that it would effect an improvement for much of the area concerned, but the Pier & Harbour Commissioners, who were responsible for the Royal Pier and the Town Quay were reluctant to agree to the proposed tramway being worked by steam locomotives, they were in favour of horses being used.

The 1895 building on the Commercial Road side of Southampton West station as it appeared during the early years of the present century. Horse drawn vehicles are very much in evidence. The road on the left leads to the level crossing and the water front.   *Author's collection*

A Waterloo–Bournemouth Pullman car express train just south of Swaythling station about 1900. The third coach is a Pullman car. The LSWR first introduced Pullman cars on their Waterloo to Bournemouth services on 21st April 1890. Two cars were initially provided – *Duchess of Albany* and *Duchess of Fife*, while in 1893 two more cars – *Duchess of Connaught* and *Princess Margaret* were brought into service. These two cars were assembled at Eastleigh Carriage Works from parts supplied by the Pullman Car Company. For several years four trains each way daily contained a single car, but from 1907 the Pullmans were gradually replaced by dining cars, the last of the Pullmans being withdrawn in 1912. The line in the foreground is the shunting neck for the small goods yard which was on the 'down' side at Swaythling. The locomotive No. 297 is one of Drummond's C8 class completed in 1898. *Author's collection*

Mainly as a result of the attitude of the Commissioners it was eventually decided that the connection with the LSWR would be made by way of a tunnel under the town. To take the place of the proposed station near the Royal Pier a station would be provided at Blechynden (West End).

The Act authorising the construction of the Southampton & Dorchester Railway was given the Royal Assent on 21st July 1845, the line from Southampton to Redbridge to be double track, and the rest of the line to Dorchester would be single with passing loops at stations. The connection to be made with the LSWR at Northam to be facing for trains from the LSWR terminus, so that all trains from and to London had to proceed via that station. This junction later became known as Southampton junction (Bevois Street Crossing).

The construction of the tunnel did not prove easy, and was not helped by the existence of the old Salisbury Canal tunnel which crossed obliquely the line of the new tunnel. The *Hampshire Advertiser* for the 2nd May 1846 reported that the excavations for the tunnel commenced in West Magdalens field on 25th April. Cuttings were first made and then covered over to form the tunnel and in October 1846 the *Hampshire Advertiser* reported that despite the treacherous soil the work was progressing well, but a num-

ber of men worked by night and the effect of the fires in the deep cuttings created a most notable effect. The nature of the soil, however, continued to give trouble for by March 1847 a number of miners from Cornwall had been specially engaged to complete the work. On 23rd April 1847 a considerable quantity of earth fell in the tunnel and according to newspaper reports there were a few men in the tunnel at the time, and details of the damage was quoted as "the footpath and a great deal of earth all around were carried into the gulf. The London Road (now Above Bar Street) which at the spot passes over the tunnel, has sunk considerably during the work and the fissures and the sinking of the road just below where it crosses over the long disused tunnel of the Salisbury Canal, indicated considerable danger, so the Commissioners of Improvement have therefore very properly stopped the traffic on the road".

The necessary repairs were completed, and on 20th May 1847, Captain Coddington, the Government Inspector of Railways, made an official inspection of the railway and spent some two or three hours in the tunnel carefully examining the work. Official notice was given that the line would be open for traffic on 1st June 1847.

On Sunday 30th May further trouble was experienced and although the line fron Blechynden to Dorchester was opened on the advertised date, trains started from and

Northam Quay – where the coal for the coke ovens at Northam was unloaded. For many years the Quay was used for unloading material for Dixon & Carlus' Mill which was adjacent to the Wharf. One of their locomotives, either *Eva* or *Nicholson* is shown here shunting on the quayside. *Southern Evening Echo*

terminated at Blechynden, and there was no through working with the London & South Western Railway. The *Hampshire Advertiser* for 5th June reported that to enable the trains to operate it was necessary for some of the engines and carriages to be conveyed by an immense team of horses through the street of the town from the London & South Western station to Blechynden. The repairs to the tunnel were completed by 29th July 1847 after which through working between the two companies was commenced.

It was agreed that the LSWR would work the line , paying an annual rent of £20,000 and sharing the profits. This arrangement did not last for long for on 22nd July 1848 the Southampton & Dorchester Company was amalgamated with the LSWR.

Further Developments

An extension was made from the LSWR terminus to the Town Quay passing along the public roadway outside the Dock Company's boundary. This was completed on 31st December 1847 and no doubt at the request of the Pier & Harbour Commissioners, the line was worked by horses. Two wagon turntables were provided, one in Canute Road immediately outside the LSWR terminus and the other at the entrance to the Town Quay.

In 1848 Waterloo station was opened and Nine Elms subsequently became the Company's principal Goods Depot for the London area.

On 2nd August 1858 a new spur was brought into use at Northam, the connection being about 400 yards north of the original connection between the LSWR and the Southampton & Dorchester Railway, thus making the triangle at Northam and giving direct running between London and Dorchester. The curvature of the new lines was very sharp which necessitated a permanent speed restriction of 7 m.p.h. being imposed. In 1907 this was raised to 15 m.p.h. and in the 1970s the curvature was eased enabling the restriction to be raised to 25 m.p.h. At first this new spur was not used by passenger trains to any great extent as the majority continued to pass via the LSWR terminus, then the principal station in the town.

The next step in the development of the railways of Southampton occurred in 1861 when an Act was passed authorising the construction of the Southampton & Netley Railway. Further Acts were passed on 22nd June 1863 and 14th July 1864, the line being eventually opened to the public on 5th March 1866.

Trials were given to a block signalling system on the Windsor line in 1865 and as this proved successful, it was decided to introduce a similar system between Bishopstoke (later Eastleigh) and Southampton. This was the start of what became the regular practice for the signalling of trains for many years.

In 1867 the construction of a large hotel round the south end of the LSWR terminus was completed and was originally known as the Imperial Hotel, but within a few years it was renamed the South Western Hotel. The building remains today as South Western House.

In 1871 the line at Southampton Town Quay was

Southampton Town Quay on 2nd August 1957. Class C14 No. 30588 in a slightly incongruous setting with other types of vehicles.
The late E.R. Morten

extended on to the Royal Pier and a passenger train service, worked initially by horse drawn coaches, was introduced between the terminus station and the Royal Pier.

In the 1880s the Didcot, Newbury & Southampton Railway were planning to reach Southampton from the Shirley direction, and the Company planned to erect a new station at the west end of the Bargate Street (approximately on the site of the main entrance to Pirelli General Cable Works in Western Esplanade). This would have necessitated carrying the Didcot, Newbury & Southampton Railway over the LSWR on a series of arches just west of the mouth of the tunnel. The work on some of these arches was commenced just north of Commercial Road, but the scheme was later abandoned with the connection with the LSWR being made at Shawford Junction, although the remains of the arches and embankments could be found for many years. To oppose the Didcot, Newbury & Southampton Railway Company's plans the LSWR put forward in 1881/2 a scheme for a railway from Southampton West along the Western Esplanade ending at a proposed new pier near the Royal Pier.

During the 1880s Southampton Dock Company were experiencing difficulties in providing sufficient funds to finance the proposed Empress Dock and the Dock Company, with the sanction of Parliament, entered into an agreement with the LSWR for a loan of £250,000. This enabled the Empress Dock to be completed in 1890, but it did not considerably improve the financial position of the

Dock Company and subsequent discussions resulted in the LSWR taking over the Southampton Dock Company as from 1st November 1892, thus obtaining complete control of Southampton Docks, the purchase price being £1,360,000. What had been proposed in 1831 being finally achieved – railways and docks under one ownership.

The LSWR continued to develop the port – the American Line transferred their North Atlantic service from Liverpool in 1893, and peacetime troopships were operating from Southampton from 1895 – all producing additional traffic and revenue for the railway. The experience gained proved useful in dealing with extra traffic in connection with the South African War of 1899–1902, during which time nearly nine hundred troopships were dealt with involving the provision of many special trains.

During the 1870s the arches in the embankment between just south of St. Denys and Mount Pleasant were filled in and the reclamation of the mudlands was commenced in 1886. In 1893 twenty seven acres of land was purchased from Bevois Park Estate for £13,200. On 16th September 1901 Bevois Park sidings were brought into use.

On 22nd February 1902 an additional up line between Mount Pleasant Crossing and St. Denys was brought into use and on 16th March 1902 a new up local line between Northam Junction and Mount Pleasant Crossing was completed thus providing two up lines between Northam Junction and St. Denys. On 4th May 1902 a new down local line was brought into use between St. Denys and

A view of the damage caused to the 'up' side buildings at Southampton Central as a result of an air raid on 23rd November 1940. The building on the left of the photograph was the Docks & Marine Sports Club opened in 1937 and destroyed in a later air raid.

Author's collection

Northam Junction and the existing down line became the down through line.

With the opening of the new motive power depot at Eastleigh on 1st January 1903 the locomotive depot which existed at Northam on the downside of the line just south of Mount Pleasant Crossing was closed and it was demolished by the end of 1903 the area eventually being developed as another goods marshalling yard finally completed in 1923.

First World War Activities

The additional military traffic handled during the South African war was only a preliminary to the massive traffic dealt with during the First World War. In August 1914 Southampton became No.1 Military Embarkation port. The number of trains passing in and out of the docks was such that the level crossings at Mount Pleasant, Bevois Street, Chapel and Canute Road were completely closed to all road traffic for the duration of the war. In 1917 a train ferry jetty was constructed west of the Royal Pier and the rail connection to this jetty was made from the West station. The train ferry and the jetty were operated by the Military Docks & Inland Waterways and were never used for commercial purposes.

Formation of the Southern Railway

As from 1st January 1923 the LSWR became part of Southern Railway. In January 1928 alterations were made to the goods lines between Northam and Southampton Terminus to provide for two additional running lines between Southampton Junction (Bevois Street Crossing) and the Terminus for traffic to and from Southampton Old Docks (now known as Eastern Docks). By the end of the 1920s work had started on the construction of the New Docks (now known as Western Docks) and in conjunction with the work the line from the Town Quay was extended across the front of the Royal Pier to the new site.

Direct access to the New Docks was to be made at Millbrook, and in order to cope with the anticipated additional traffic it was decided to provide two additional running lines between Southampton and Millbrook and also to enlarge Southampton West station (renamed Southampton Central in July 1935) with the provision of two additional platform lines and a new building on the downside of the station. In connection with the provision of the additional lines a Contractor's siding, known as Jackaman's siding, was laid in during August 1931 on the downside of the line at the Redbridge end of Millbrook station. The new work was brought into use in June 1935.

Nicely framed by the signal gantry, Merchant Navy class No. 35021 *New Zealand Line* on an 'up' Bournemouth to Waterloo train approaching Southampton Central on 26th July 1951.   *L. Elsey*

'Q' class 0-6-0 No. 30542 on a 'down' freight train passing through Swaythling station on 2nd August 1957.   *The late E.R. Morten*

A rare sight in the south, 'A4' No. 60024 *Kingfisher* on an 'A4 Preservation Society' railtour to Weymouth running between Southampton Central and Millbrook on 26th March 1966.   *M.J. Fox*

Second World War

With the outbreak of war in September 1939 the Docks became the supply bridgehead for the British Expeditionary force. The railway suffered during the many air–raids on the town – the major damage occurring at Southampton Central when part of the downside building was completely destroyed. Various warehouses in the Docks were damaged beyond repair. The port, however, became one of the major embarkation points for the final invasion of Europe in 1944, and throughout the whole period 4.3 million officers and men passed through the port together with 3.9 million tons of stores and equipment.

British Railways

Under nationalisation the Southern Railway became the Southern Region of British Railways as from 1st January 1948 and under the 1962 Transport Act Southampton Docks was finally divorced from the railways with the abolition of the British Transport Commission and the formation of the British Transport Docks Board, which became an independent statutory authority.

1957 saw the introduction of the very successful diesel electric multiple units on many of the local services in the Southampton area. Some of these units are still operating today, although with the recent extension of electrification in the area these units are likely to be completely withdrawn.

Over the years Southampton Tunnel has given the Engineer's Department many problems and from time to time major repairs have been necessary involving only one line being available for trains passing through the tunnel. Such work was carried out between November 1964 and March 1965 and again between March 1983 and July 1985.

The Beeching era of rail closures had little effect on the stations of Southampton, ten stations were still open, but when plans for electrification were considered it was decided to close Northam and Southampton Terminus and this took effect from 5th September 1966.

Electrification

Electric services commenced operating in the Southampton area in April 1967 and the full electric service between Waterloo and Bournemouth came into operation on 10th

Battle of Britain class No. 34071 *601 Squadron* on an 'up' Bournemouth to Waterloo train in January 1967. Reconstruction of the buildings on the 'up' side is under way and access to the platform was gained through the temporary covered way on the right. In the background, on the right, the building which housed the District Traffic Supt's staff still stands. *The late J.R. Fairman collection*

July 1967. In connection with this programme further development took place at Southampton Central station where the upside building of 1895 was demolished and replaced by the present four storey office block which came into use in 1968.

With the development of containerisation a Freightliner Terminal was established at Millbrook in January 1968 and four years later the Maritime Terminal located to the rear of the container berths in the Western Docks was brought into use. With the decline in passenger liner movements the number of boat trains operating to and from Southampton Docks has since 1970 considerably declined and with much of the general cargo passing in containers the need for an extensive rail network serving the Docks was no longer necessary. In March 1980 the down line between Northam Junction and Canute Road was taken out of use and the up line converted to a single line – now the sole remaining railway link with the Old (Eastern) Docks. In 1987 approximately 60% of all the containers passing through the port were dealt with by Freightliner so British Railways are still well into the business of moving shipping traffic so far as Southampton is concerned.

A new station with a Southampton name, but not within the city boundary, was opened in the area on 1st April 1966 – Southampton Airport (Eastleigh) provided entirely for passengers travelling to and from Southampton/Eastleigh Airport. The station was built on the site of Atlantic Park Halt, which was opened in the late 1920s for dealing with European immigrants who were accommodated at Atlantic Park (now Southampton/Eastleigh Airport) waiting clearance to enter America. The Halt then consisted of one short platform on the downside of the line only. In 1986 Southampton Airport (Eastleigh) station was

re-developed and on 29th September of that year was renamed Southampton Parkway and made available to all passengers. A ticket office was built on the up platform and a large car park, spaces now being provided for 300 cars, was constructed on the upside, partly on land owned by the railway for many years, originally scheduled for the provision of four lines of railway between Eastleigh and St. Denys. This car park is often full making Southampton Parkway a very busy passenger station.

At one time there were fifteen signal boxes in the area and even in the mid 1960s there were still nine operational boxes, but between October 1981 and February 1982 colour light signalling together with track circuit block working was extended to cover the whole of the Southampton area, resulting in the complete elimination of all the remaining signal boxes. Thw whole area is now under the control of Eastleigh signal box. To improve the general train running the lines between Northam Junction and Southampton were converted in November 1981 for reversible working, i.e., trains could pass in either direction on either line. This arrangement also applied to all running lines through the platforms at Southampton and also on the down and up fast lines to Millbrook.

In 1988 new rolling stock appeared on many of the services in the Southampton area including the Wessex (442 class) electric units on the Waterloo to Weymouth route, and Sprinters (155, 156 and 158 classes) on the cross country services between Portsmouth and Bristol and Cardiff. Electrification of the lines between St. Denys and Fareham was completed in May 1990. More passengers are travelling by rail, so the railways in Southampton are still very much alive after 150 years of serving the area.

Swaythling

A Railway Companion published in 1839 makes reference to Swaythling as follows:- " ... our train puffs on to Swathling station, near where the Romsey and Southampton turnpike roads join". This was, however, mainly in the imagination of the writer of the Guide, for when the railway was being planned a station was mooted, but when the line between Winchester and Northam was opened in 1839, there was no station at Swaythling. In fact it was forty four years later when the present station was opened on 15th October 1883. When the station was opened about twenty trains called daily. The date 1883 can

still be clearly seen on the front of the main station building located on the downside of the line. The spelling of the station name was originally 'Swathling' – the 'y' being added in July 1895.

The station, which was constructed by the then well known local builders J. Bull & Sons, is of somewhat unusual construction for the main station building is separated from the down platform by a short covered corridor. The reason for this was that at some time in the future it was the intention to provide additional running lines through the station, and if this had come about all that would have been

Above: Swaythling station looking north showing the 'down' side station building of 1883. The connecting corridor between the building the 'down' platform is hidden behind a bush. The pathway in the right foreground leads from the footbridge which is also a public right of way over the railway.   *Cosser*

Right: Swaythling looking very busy with a 'down' passenger train and plenty of staff in attendance during the early part of the present century. The rolling stock is typical LSWR – three coaches each 48 feet in length and a six wheeled brake van. Various combinations existed and the second vehicle has 3rd and 2nd class compartments – the word 'Second' can be seen on one of the open doors. It is interesting to note that this coach still has the gas lighting fittings on the roof.   *Author's collection*

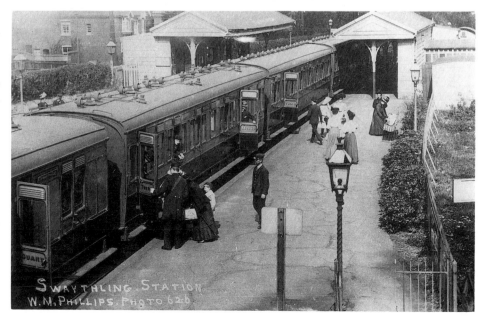

Above: Drummond's 'T9' No. 296 heads a 'down' train passing through Swaythling – the corridor linking the 'down' platform and the station building can be clearly seen. Very typical of railways in the earlier days, an old coach body has been utilised for use as a Parcels/Goods Shed.

D. Cullum collection

Below: About the turn of the century Drummond's 'T9' No. 704 (built in 1899) hauls a special train through Swaythling. Over the top of the fourth coach can be seen the roof of Swaythling signal box.

Author's collection

Swaythling signal box on the 'up' side of the line just south of the station – a typical LSWR signal box with the large roof ventilators and the fire buckets on the veranda. It was closed in 1966.   *P.R. Moody*

necessary was to rebuild the down platform without affecting the station building. In fact powers to provide additional lines were first obtained in 1900, but the work was not authorised and during the mid 1920s plans were prepared for two additional lines to be provided throughout from Eastleigh to link up with the four lines already existing just south of St. Denys, but these plans never came to fruition, and with the later development of colour light signalling it was found not to be necessary.

A small goods yard existed on the downside of the line at the Southampton end of the station, consisting of two yard sidings and a loading dock with a short shunting neck running parallel with the down line towards St. Denys. On 24th December 1914 an additional siding together with a platform was brought into use at the back of the goods yard, the running line connection for this siding being from the down line near Woodmill Lane road overbridge. This siding was for the Army Remount Depot and trains conveying horses, which were eventually shipped to France during the First World War, were regularly dealt with on this siding. The connection was removed on 16th October 1923.

The station building would not have been in existence today if a large bomb, which went through the booking office during the evening of 19th January 1941, had exploded. It killed the dog belonging to the leading porter

and made quite a mess of the office. The ARP authorities decided that the bomb had exploded and the office remained in use. The next day the landlord of the Masons Arms opposite the station expressed the opinion that the bomb had not exploded, and the office was evacuated while the Bomb Disposal staff began digging for the bomb. It was not until a fortnight afterwards that they removed it.

Freight train services were withdrawn on 13th July 1959 and the sidings in the goods yard were removed in October 1961. The majority of the land is at present occupied by Vincent Self Drive Vehicles.

The footbridge at the south end of the platform also serves as a public right of way from Wessex Lane to High Road. The present iron footbridge was erected in 1883, with the opening of the station , and took the place of a wooden bridge.

The signal box which existed at the Southampton end of the up platform was typical of many LSWR signal boxes with the large roof ventilator. The box was equipped with a nineteen lever Stevens frame and was taken out of use on 6th November 1966.

Between Swaythling and St. Denys for many years Woodmill Intermediate signal box existed on the downside of the line near Kent Road Sewage Works. The box, which was very small, was closed on 9th December 1930 when intermediate section signals were brought into use.

Above: Drummond's 'K10' No. 345 on a Waterloo–Alton–Southampton Terminus train passing over Kent Road bridge, Portswood, during the early part of the century. To the rear of the train can be seen a rare view of Woodmill signal box which was closed in 1930 being replaced by intermediate section signals operated from Swaythling and St. Denys. *Author's collection*
Below: On a misty January morning in 1964 Merchant Navy class No. 35016 *Elders & Fyffes* with an 'up' Bournemouth to Waterloo train storms through Swaythling. *P.J. Cupper*

St. Denys

In 1857 the inhabitants of Portswood, Highfield and Bevois Valley prepared a memorial to the LSWR in favour of a station near the road bridge in St. Denys Road, and it was stated that the inhabitants were being inconvenienced by the great distance from the Town station. In the following year it was decided to provide a station at Portswood and Mr. Edwin Jones made a present of an area of land just north of the St. Denys Road bridge. The work of constructing platforms for short trains was commenced at the end of October 1858, but the station was not officially opened until 29th April 1861, then being named Portswood.

necessary by the similarity between Portswood and Portsmouth, but this is a little surprising as the branch line then only went as far as Netley and the route from Southampton to Portsmouth was via Bishopstoke (now Eastleigh).

The line from Netley was extended to Fareham in 1889 but remained a single line with crossing loops. Major alterations were carried out at St. Denys in 1899. The down platform was made into an island platform while a new branch platform was provided together with additional lines to and from Netley, the junction being moved to the south end of the station. In March 1899 a new signal box was built at Dukes Road level crossing adjoining the crossing

St. Denys – looking south from the Island platform – a familiar sight for many years – the tall signal posts with the lower quadrant signals, with a duplicate arm for the 'down' through line lower down the post. The two ringed arm signals gave access to Bevois Park sidings. These signal posts were replaced in 1955 by a gantry with upper quadrant signals. St. Denys signal box can be seen on the 'up' side immediately behind the main line post and beyond that the 'Horseshoe Bridge' linking Dukes Road with Priory Road.   *John Bailey*

It did not remain very long on that site, for with the opening of the line to Netley on 5th March 1866, a new station with up and down platforms was opened on its present site, and the station buildings then constructed on the up platform still remain today. The railway to Netley was originally a single line and the junction with the main line was at the north end of the down platform, a signal box existing at the north end of the up platform immediately opposite the junction. The station was still named Portswood and was not renamed St. Denys until March 1876. According to the *Southampton Times* the alteration was made

keeper's house. Shortly afterwards the Corporation were planning to extend their tram service to cover Bitterne Park and it was proposed that the tram track would pass over the railway main line on the level at Dukes Road crossing and then on into Adelaide Road, crossing the single line to Fareham, but the Board of Trade refused permission for the crossing at Dukes Road. As a result the Corporation were most anxious for a bridge to be built and they entered into an agreement for the LSWR to meet the cost of the new bridge providing the Corporation agreed to the LSWR laying additional lines over Canute Road into the Docks

One of the very last 'S15s' in service, No. 30824, passes through St. Denys after starting out of Bevois Park Yard with a special freight train for Nine Elms on 28th June 1965.

M.J. Fox

Above: St. Denys – 'U' class No. 31639 with a train from Portsmouth on 26th June 1954 – the tall signals were replaced by a gantry during the following year. *Below:* The driver of Drummond 'T9' No. 30726 waits at St. Denys for the guard's green flag with St. Denys 'down' branch starting signal and Bitterne 'down' distant signal underneath in the 'off' position on 26th June 1954. Adelaide Crossing box can be seen.

Both J.H.W. Kent

which existed immediately outside the signal box at the end of the up local line, the scene of several derailments over the years, particularly during the 1950s.

The footbridge at St. Denys station was erected in 1883, and at the request of Southampton Corporation who had received complaints from local residents that there was no means of crossing the line, it was so constructed that members of the public could use it without going on to the platforms. The bridge was extended eastwards over the additional Netley Branch lines in 1899. In 1987 with the construction of the Swaythling bypass a further extension of the bridge was carried over the bypass to give pedestrian access to the station from Osborne Road. The direct road access to the upside buildings from Osborne Road was abolished, but a new roadway and a small car park was constructed on the Northam side of the station building.

The extension of the colour light signalling and track circuit block working controlled from Eastleigh panel box resulted in the signal box being taken out of use on 11th October 1981. The building was subsequently demolished. At Adelaide Road Crossing the gates were replaced by lifting barriers on 26th June 1966, and on 11th October 1981 closed circuit television operation from the Eastleigh Box was introduced resulting in the complete demolition of the crossing box to allow for the positioning of the television cameras.

In connection with the electrification of the Netley line alterations were made in 1990 to the accommodation on the island platform, and a ticket office was provided there. This resulted in the 1866 building on the up platform being taken out of operational use.

St. Denys is served by the stopping services between Waterloo and Southampton and those between Wareham and Portsmouth Harbour.

and that the Corporation would remove the tram track in Canute Road leading to the Floating Bridge, which passed across the railway tracks. The Corporation had already obtained permission to lay new tram tracks over the Central Bridge to the Floating Bridge.

The road overbridge linking Dukes Road with Priory Road/Adelaide Road (commonly known as the Horseshoe bridge) was opened in April 1904, and the level crossing was closed on 6th April 1904. The foundation stone for this bridge was laid on 28th October 1902 and can still be seen at rail level in the brick support on the western side of the bridge. After getting the bridge built it was decided not to run the trams via Dukes Road and Adelaide Road.

The portion of line between St. Denys and Bitterne was doubled in February 1910, and Adelaide Road signal box then ceased to be a block signalling box, but remained for the operation of the level crossing gates.

For many years a bookstall existed on the up main platform at St. Denys, there was a small goods yard on the upside at the London end of the station consisting of two sidings. The points leading to these sidings were controlled from a ground frame. From 1921 until 1969 there was a small loading platform in the yard serving the Depot of Crawford & Sons, the biscuit people. The goods yard was taken out of use on 14th July 1969, and the track was removed in September of that year. Early in 1967 the gas lighting on the station was replaced by electric lighting.

During April and May 1975 alterations to the layout at the Southampton end of the station were carried out to improve the working, and as a result it was possible for a train on the up local line from Mount Pleasant Crossing to pass on to the up main line at the same time as a train travelling on the up through line was passing to the Netley line. This work also involved the abolition of the sand drag

Right: St. Denys signal box photographed near the end of its days on 18th April 1981. When the box was erected on this site in 1899 it adjoined the crossing keeper's house which was demolished in the 1960s.   *John Scrace*

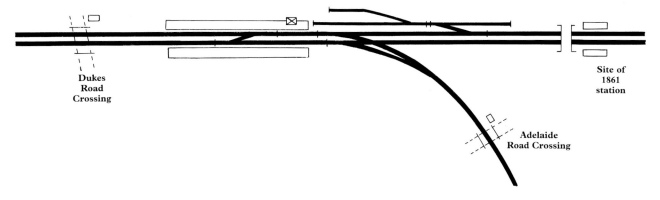

**Dukes
Road
Crossing**

**Site of
1861
station**

**Adelaide
Road Crossing**

1905

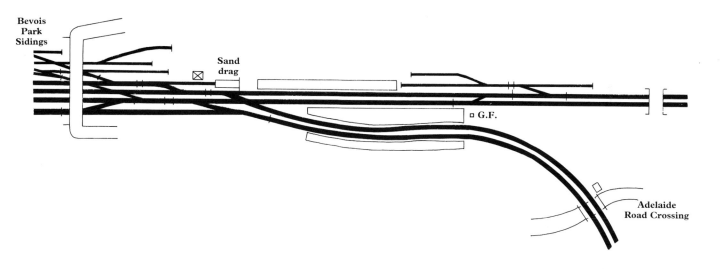

**Bevois
Park
Sidings**

**Sand
drag**

□ G.F.

**Adelaide
Road Crossing**

1976

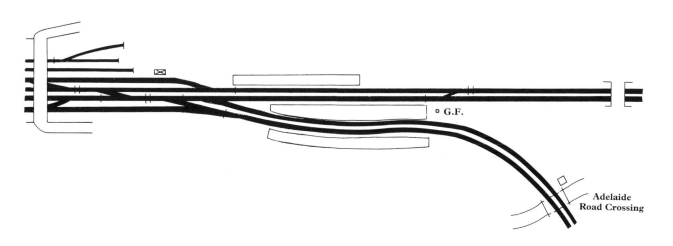

□ G.F.

**Adelaide
Road Crossing**

Drawn by
Amanda Yektaparast

ST. DENYS – The Changing Layout

Above: The 'down' 'Bournemouth Belle' with No. 35019 *French Line* passes through St. Denys on 14th May 1955. *D.H. Cull*
Below: Merchant Navy class No. 35008 *Orient Line* on a Bournemouth–Waterloo train passing St. Denys on 16th August 1962.
The line on the right of the engine is the shunting neck for the small goods yard. *L. Elsey*

Bevois Park Sidings

No. 33027 *Earl Mountbatten of Burma* on a Bristol to Portsmouth Harbour service passing through St. Denys on 14th May 1988, the last day of locomotive hauled services between Cardiff/Bristol and Portsmouth Harbour. They were replaced by class 155 Sprinters.   *I.J. Bovey*

Bevois Park sidings were brought into use on 16th September 1901, and at the same time Mount Pleasant Siding, which was adjacent to the running lines, and possibly also known as Nicholls siding, was taken out of use as the land was required for the provision of additional running lines between St. Denys and Northam. Road access to the sidings was from Imperial Road, while rail access could be gained from either the Mount Pleasant Crossing end or from St. Denys. The accommodation was quickly fully used and the need for additional sidings soon became apparent, and the yard was enlarged in 1907.

A stranger – Stanier Class '5' No. 45046 based at Crewe South working the 06.22 Bournemouth Central to Waterloo on 28th June 1965 and passing the 1903/4 built bridge just south of St. Denys. Apparently the locomotive had arrived at Weymouth on a pigeon special from the Midlands and was 'borrowed' by the Southern Region. It returned on the 15.35 Waterloo to Bournemouth on the same day and worked both services for several days before returning to the London Midland Region.
M.J. Fox

During the First World War one siding was extended across Empress Road to serve the Steel Joist Company's yard where gun carriages were being manufactured.

In 1933 various alterations were made to increase the length of some of the sidings, while others were removed. During the Second World War two additional sidings were

laid in. At one time a private siding served the warehouse of Cadbury/Fry and this siding was removed in 1962. With the general decline in ordinary freight traffic rationalisation took place in 1968, when at least nine sidings were removed, but following this a car train terminal was established. Traffic dealt with through this terminal has

fluctuated considerably over the years, but for some time Toleman's Delivery Service loaded Ford Transit vans from Ford's Works at Eastleigh.

In the 1970s Tunnel Cement Company established a depot in Bevois Park and regularly received cement from their works in Aberthaw. In 1979 approximately 90,000 tonnes in presflo wagons were dealt with, while in 1980 the Rugby Portland Cement Company, who had been operating from Northam sidings, developed a new unloading point together with a large cement silo adjacent to the

Tunnel Cement Company's depot, and for several years they regularly received cement from their works in Halling in Kent. This traffic ceased to pass for a short period, but by the end of 1989 Rugby Portland Cement Company were receiving at least one train of cement wagons each week. This has now ceased to pass.

The general decline in normal full load freight traffic in recent years has had its effect on Bevois Park Depot, and as from the spring of 1990 some full load traffic passing has been dealt with at Millbrook Freightliner Terminal.

Above: An unidentified Schools class locomotive on a Waterloo to Lymington Pier Saturdays only service, approaching Mount Pleasant Crossing, with Bevois Park sidings in the background. *The late Deryk Pye*

Left: 'M7' class No. 30029 approaching Mount Pleasant Crossing with a train for Southampton Terminus on 8th August 1953. *L. Elsey*

Mount Pleasant Crossing box of the 1890s in April 1981 with part of one of the lifting barriers which had been installed by that time.

John Scrace

Mount Pleasant Crossing

In 1893 an agreement was made between Southampton Corporation and the LSWR for the latter to lay two additional lines of rails across Mount Pleasant Crossing and to erect adjacent to the crossing a signal box equipped with 'mechanical and lever power for the proper and efficient working of the level crossing gates'. In addition a footbridge was to be erected.

Unfortunately before the box could be erected there was a fatal accident on the crossing on 21st June 1894 when the 11.40 a.m. from Waterloo struck a bread cart the driver of the cart being killed. The Gateman was committed for trial on a charge of manslaughter. It was stated at the trial that the normal practice was for the Gateman to receive a bell warning from Swaythling as the train passed, but he waited until he received a warning from St. Denys before operating the gates. The Gateman was acquitted, but the LSWR were blamed for the inadequacy of the arrangements. It was then stated that the replacement of the gates by modern ones worked by levers was being carried out.

The footbridge was brought into use in October 1894, but the construction of the somewhat large signal box on the upside of the line on the Northam side of the level crossing took longer. The two additional lines agreed to in 1893 were eventually brought into use in 1902. The four gates provided were exceptionally large as when they were open to the road they each had to extend across two lines. At times the signalman at Mount Pleasant Crossing had difficulty in operating these gates when strong winds were blowing, and an electric motor was eventually installed to assist with their operation.

The large gates were replaced by lifting barriers on 2nd July 1967, and the signal box was taken out of use on 11th October 1981 when closed circuit television operation of the barriers from Eastleigh box was introduced, and as a result of this installation it was necessary for the box to be immediately demolished to allow for the positioning of the t.v. cameras.

Above: Northam locomotive Depot, on the left, during the last few years of its life. Drummond's 'T9' No. 706 (completed in 1899) passes the Depot with a special 'up' London train. The line on the right is believed to be Mount Pleasant Siding, also known as Nicholl's siding. Soon after this picture was taken the siding and the loading platform were removed to allow for the provision of an additional 'up' line between Northam Junction and Mount Pleasant Crossing which was brought into use as the 'up' local line on 16th March 1902. It would seem that the signal post was newly erected having a post for the 'up' local line and one for the connection to Bevois Park sidings opened in September 1901. The Locomotive depot was closed on 1st January 1903 following the opening of the Depot at Eastleigh. *D. Cullum collection*

Below: LSWR 4-4-2T No. 421, built by Beyer Peacock & Company in 1882, stands outside the south end of Northam locomotive shed. The locomotive was scrapped in 1921. *C.H. Eden*

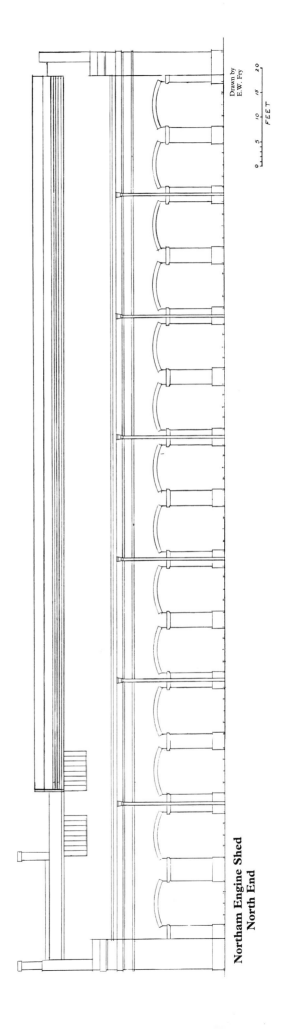

Northam Engine Shed
North End

Drawn by
E.W. Fry

0 5 10 15 20
FEET

One of Joseph Beattie's Falcon class 2-4-0s *Sultana* stands outside Northam Shed. The engine was built in 1866 at Nine Elms and was withdrawn from service in 1884.

Author's collection

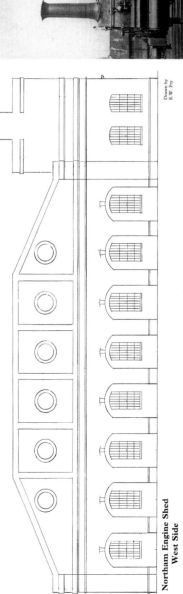

Northam Engine Shed
West Side

Drawn by
E.W. Fry

Layout of Northam Engine Shed 1870

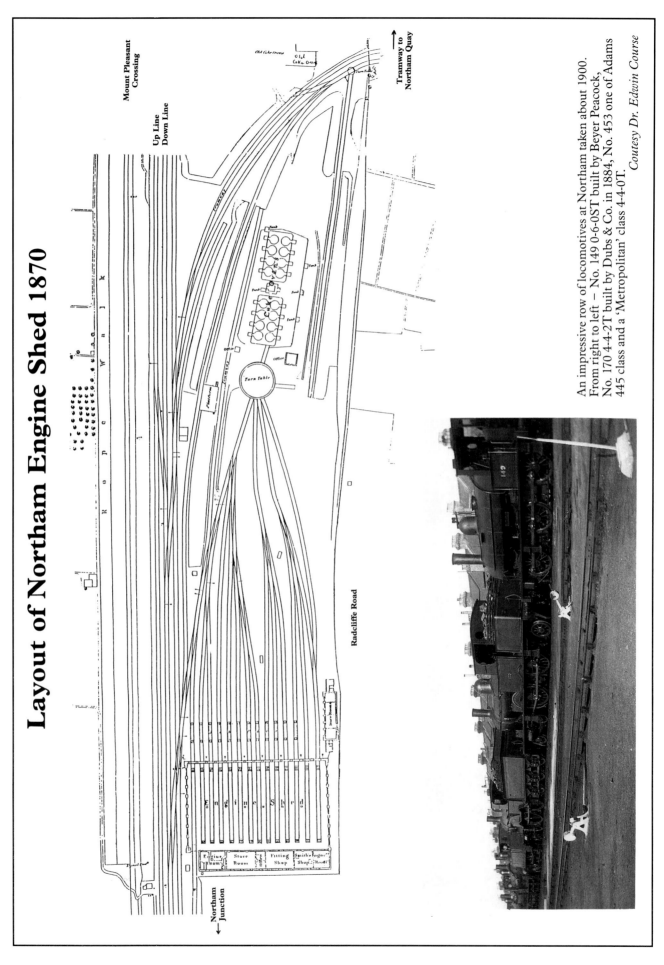

Mount Pleasant
Crossing

Up Line
Down Line

Old Coke Ovens
Old
Coke Oven

Tramway to
Northam Quay

R o p e W a l k

Turn Table

Platform

Office

Office

Engine Shed

Radcliffe Road

Fitting
Shop

Store
Room

Smiths Engine
Shop House

Northam
Junction

An impressive row of locomotives at Northam taken about 1900. From right to left – No. 149 0-6-0ST built by Beyer Peacock, No. 170 4-4-2T built by Dubs & Co. in 1884, No. 453 one of Adams 445 class and a 'Metropolitan' class 4-4-0T.

Coutesy Dr. Edwin Course

Northam

One of the then last remaining King Arthur class locomotives No. 30788 *Sir Urre of the Mount* strides northwards from Northam with a banana special from Southampton Docks on 24th April 1961. On the left an unidentified diesel shunter is working in Northam Yard. The splendid row of lower quadrant signals on the gantry carrying the 'down' home signals for Northam Junction is shown at its best.

P.J. Cupper

In the late 1860s various requests from the inhabitants in the Northam area were made to the LSWR for a station to be provided near 'The Old Farm Gate' (known as Mount Pleasant Crossing) as – "the inhabitants were being inconvenienced by the great distance to reach the Town (LSWR terminus) station". In 1870, a Mr. Alfred James Dyer raised considerable interest in the scheme to provide a station at Northam bridge, and he eventually created so much agitation that the Railway Company decided to erect the station on that site. The station was opened on Sunday 1st December 1872, (I wonder how many other stations were opened on a Sunday), and the local papers reported that some flags were displayed in the neighbourhood on the following day.

The citizens of the Northam area showed their appreciation of Mr. Dyer's efforts in no uncertain terms for on the 2nd December a dinner was held in his honour at the South Western Hotel, when he was presented with a silver ink-stand and a purse containing at least fifty sovereigns.

Despite being provided at the junction, the platforms were constructed to serve only the lines to and from the LSWR terminus. When the station was opened a staff of eight were provided, and all down passenger trains were booked to stop at Northam for ticket examination, and this enabled the ticket platform near the LSWR terminus to be removed. The station was constructed by the local builders J. Bull & Sons who were associated with the construction of various other railway works in the area. The station offices were of wooden construction at road level, being approximately over the London end of the up (to London)

platform. Access to the platforms was gained by separate entrances from the road bridge with a set of steps leading to each platform.

The *Southampton Times* suggested that the station buildings could eventually cover the area of land then known as the 'Triangle', and as the piece of land opposite the Glebe Hotel (renamed the Queen Vic in 1988) in Northam Road was the property of the Railway Company, this would constitute a very good approach to the bridge which might be erected across the Dorchester line, and cabs would thus be able to obtain access to the platforms.

Northam station looking north about 1900. Northam junction signal box was then located on the 'down' side of the line and can be clearly seen through the bridge. The building at the back of the signal box is part of Mulford Brothers timber yard.

S.U.I.A.G.

Above: Dubs built 0-6-0 No. 697 working a troop train through Northam station to Southampton Docks, possibly during the Boer War, but prior to 1908 when the road overbridge in the background was rebuilt. *D. Cullum collection*

Below: Northam station from the 'down' platform looking north prior to the reconstruction of the road over bridge in 1908. The station offices were at road level and separate steps existed to gain access to each platform. *Lens of Sutton*

Looking north from the footbridge at Southampton Junction on 28th June 1964. The lines on the left are the original link between the London & Southampton Railway and the Southampton and Dorchester Railway. Centre are the lines to and from St. Denys and the lines on the right – known as Nos. 1 and 2 sidings which ran behind the 'down' platform at Northam and connected Northam yard with Chapel sidings and Southampton Goods Shed.

Bert Moody

It is of interest that the piece of land referred to was never developed and it is now a site for advertisement hoardings although behind them is an electricity sub–station.

Prior to the road bridge being completed in 1840 accommodation was provided for two resident policemen or crossing keepers. As far as can be established the accommodation was later enlarged to provide for the station master, and the house on the upside of the line just north of the road bridge remained for many years. It was finally demolished in July 1989 to make way for a new road bridge over the railway which is likely to be constructed within the next few years.

A deputation from the Council, including the Mayor, paid a visit to Waterloo in 1889 to meet officials of the Railway Company to discuss the provision of a more central railway station in the area of Northam. Nothing, however, came of this suggestion and the new West station was opened in 1895 on the site of the present Southampton station.

Discussions took place in 1904 between Southampton Council and the Railway Company for the renewal of the road bridge at Northam. The Council wanted the bridge to be forty feet wide between the parapets and the approaches and the road to be constructed suitable for an electric tramway. Agreement was eventually reached for the Council to pay a quarter of the cost of the new bridge, but the amount payable by the Council was not to exceed £5,000. To enable the new bridge to be built, a temporary road bridge was erected on the north side of the then existing bridge. The work was carried out during 1907 and 1908 and the new bridge was brought into use on 24th June 1908. This was followed by the completion of new station buildings, which were still at road level, but were

constructed on a separate girder spanning the lines to the Terminus. Then only one public entrance was provided at street level together with a footbridge, and for some time a lift existed.

The electric tramway was extended over the new road bridge to Northam river bridge in December 1910. On

Northam – reconstruction of the road overbridge in 1908. Northam Junction signal box can be seen on the 'down' side of the line. Compare this view with the previous one showing the signal box and it is obvious that some realignment of the tracks through the junction took place, and indicates that the signal box had been set back a few feet. This was done in 1901/2 in connection with the provision of an additional 'down' line between St. Denys and Northam Junction.

Author's collection

Standard class 4 2-6-0 No. 76016 leaving Northam Station with the 07.00 Reading–Southampton Terminus on 19th May 1965.
M.J. Fox

26th April 1915 the use of platform tickets, price one penny, was introduced at Northam. With the introduction of the trams, and later buses, passenger traffic slowly

Northam Junction signal box on 18th July 1974 – this box, on the 'up' side of the line just north of the junction, was brought into use in 1923. It was closed in 1981 when Eastleigh Box was extended to cover the Southampton area and the building was subsequently demolished. *John Scrace*

declined. At the TUCC held in November 1965 concerning the proposed closure of the station it was revealed that an average of 530 passengers used the station each day. The passenger service was withdrawn and the station closed on 5th September 1966.

Three signal boxes controlled the triangle at Northam, the main box being Northam Junction which was originally on the downside of the line. To allow for the provision of an additional down line between St. Denys and Northam in 1902 the box was set back clear during the year. During the same year a very large gantry carrying signals applicable to the down line was also erected. On the 8th July 1923 a new signal box was brought into use on the upside of the line. This box was fitted with a 56 lever Stevens frame and remained in use until the introduction of colour light signalling and track circuit block working in the area on 11th October 1981.

Southampton Junction controlled the south end of the triangle and was originally located on the downside south of Bevois Street level crossing, but when additional lines were provided over the crossing the box was rebuilt on the Northam side of the level crossing and was fitted with a 40 lever frame. The level crossing was closed in January 1966 and the box remained in use until 2nd October 1966 when

Above: Southampton Junction signal box on 28th June 1964 – Bevois Street level crossing had been closed in January of that year and a hand written notice to that effect is hanging on the gates. The box was soon to be closed for it was taken out of use in October 1964, but the footbridge remains in use today.
Bert Moody

Below: Class 'U' 2-6-0 No. 31808 with a Southampton Terminus–Portsmouth & Southsea train approaching Southampton Junction. The siding on the left served Chapel Tramway.
L. Elsey

Above: Chapel Crossing looking north about 1930. GWR 4-4-0 No. 3261 *St. Germans* with one of the through M. & S.W. Junction trains from Cheltenham proceeding to Southampton Terminus. In the background on the right can be seen wagons standing on Chapel sidings, which served the Gas Works etc. The two lines to the right of the locomotive are the 'up' and 'down' through lines serving Southampton (Eastern) Docks.
L. & G.R.P.

Left: Chapel Crossing signal box looking very smart on 21st July 1976 – the last crossing in the Southampton area to retain the conventional type gates which remained until October 1981, when the crossing was converted to an 'open' type crossing with flashing lights.
John Scrace

control of the whole triangle was transferred to Northan Junction box.

The west end of the Northam triangle was controlled by Southampton Tunnel Junction box which was located in the junction. It was a small high box fitted with a 14 lever frame which was at right angles to the running lines. The box was closed on the 2nd October 1966 when control of the triangle was transferred to Northam Junction box.

The original connection at Southampton Junction between the LSWR and the Southampton & Dorchester Railway was removed at the end of 1973, after being out of use for several months.

Northam station was left to decay, but in 1969 both platforms were removed and the station buildings at road level were demolished during the following year. All that remains today is a short brick wall at road level in the centre of the south side of the road bridge, where the station entrance used to be.

Southampton Terminus

Southampton Terminus station as it was known by the majority has, over the years, had various changes in its official title. When opened in 1840, being then the only station in the town it was called Southampton. This lasted until July 1858, when it was renamed Southampton Docks. In September 1896 it became Southampton Town & Docks until November 1912, when it was amended to Southampton Town for Docks. On 9th July 1923 it was renamed Southampton Terminus, and retained that name until closure in September 1966. Although there are various termini in this country, Southampton Terminus was the only one so named officially.

The land in the vicinity of the station was known as the Marsh, and an area of about six acres on which the station was constructed was conveyed by Southampton Corporation as a gift. The station building which remains today in use as a casino, was brought into use on 11th May 1840, when the railway line throughout from Nine Elms to Southampton was opened. The building was designed by Sir William Tite, and is a good example of the style characteristic of the early Victorian period. Originally only two platforms were provided together with an engine shed. The usual facilities existed in the station building including a ticket office, refreshment room, station superintendent's office, parcels office, ladies and gentlemens waiting rooms, a strong room and a porters room.

The *Hampshire Advertiser* of 7th March 1846 reported that "an immense turning table is forming at the mouth of the engine house at Southampton railway terminus sufficiently large for turning an engine and tender together".

Traffic gradually increased and by 1865 additional sidings had been provided on the east side of the station.

The Terminus station as seen from the Central Bridge in about 1896/7 emphasising how the large South Western Hotel completely overpowered the station buildings. The locomotive is a Beattie 2-4-0 and the headcode indicates that it was a local train to Salisbury, possibly the 10.18 or the 11.33. Among the carriages are several Great Western coaches and the congested state of the station suggests that storage accommodation for carriages must have been very limited. On the right in the yard in the background are several cattle trucks.
Southampton Record Office

In the late 1860s the Imperial Hotel, later to become South Western Hotel, was built on the corner of Terminus Terrace and Canute Road. By 1870 the main platform adjoining the station building was approximately 480 feet in length with a bay of about 250 feet in length at the north end. The platform opposite the main platform was about 300 feet in length. Four lines existed between the platforms and about midway along the shorter platform the lines were all linked with four coach/wagon turntables. The two centre lines also had a turntable on each line near the buffer stops. There were also three offices for Steam Packet Companies indicating the importance of shipping traffic to the railway. At the north end of the station there was a goods shed and adjoining this was a loading platform in the goods yard then located between Terminus Terrace and Bridge Road. Rail access to the yard from the running lines was gained by a series of wagon turntables, and on the edge of the yard were a row of stables – obviously horses were used for

Two photographs of the LSWR terminus taken between 1880 and 1900. The tram track exists for the horse trams, but there are no overhead wires. It will be noted that the upper windows in the building are much larger than those shown on the 1841 engraving. The arrangements of the buildings at the back of the South Western Hotel prior to the alterations and extensions of the 1920s can be clearly seen on the lower photograph.
Author's collection

Above: Southampton Terminus and adjacent goods sidings with three engines shunting, about the turn of the century.
G. Bixley collection
Right: A later view of the station with the name boards across the front of the building. It was known as Southampton Docks station from 1858 until 1896.
Author's collection

shunting in addition to road deliveries. Adjacent to the station building a Postal & Telegraph office was established, and this building remained until recent times, and the words 'Postal Telegraphs' could be clearly seen, even long after the building had ceased to be used for that purpose.

A second goods shed measuring about 160 feet by 60 feet was sited on Canute Road and adjoining this shed was a single road engine shed with a turntable immediately outside the shed.

Two level crossings existed – one serving Bridge Road and the other Marsh Lane. In 1870 the signal box was on the downside of the line on the station side of Bridge Road crossing alongside St. Lawrence Road, which was then a

public thoroughfare linking Bridge Road and Canute Road. At the Canute Road end of St. Lawrence Road there were several hotels including Hotel du Commerce, St. Lawrence Hotel and on the corner with Canute Road New York Hotel. The Royal Mail Steam Packet Company had a store in St. Lawrence Road, while their offices were then just round the corner in Canute Road. The signal box at Marsh Lane level crossing was on the upside of the line on the north side of the crossing.

The station was an "open" station in the early days and a ticket platform, about 250 feet in length, was provided for ticket examination and collection. When Northam station was opened in 1872 the ticket platform

Southampton Terminus yard and the Central Bridge – a tram is on the bridge proceeding to the Floating Bridge. This photograph taken in July 1941 shows the air raid damage which occurred to the Parcels Office and the canopy on platform Nos. 1 & 2.
Author's collection

Another view of the station – this time taken in about 1908 and shows the time ball on top of South Western Hotel. Before the days of radio, people set their watches correct for the day by waiting for the time ball, which at 09.55 (10.55 B.S.T.) each day was hoisted to the top of the pole and at 10.00 (11.00 B.S.T.) the ball, electrically released from Greenwich would slide down the pole. The arrangement ceased to operate during the 1930s.   *Southern Evening Echo*

In July 1882 Central Bridge was opened and this enabled the level crossings at Bridge Road and Marsh Lane to be closed. A metal plate, as shown, still exists on one side of the bridge, which now forms part of the approach road to the Itchen river bridge opened in 1977. It now spans only one railway track leading to and from the Old (Eastern) Docks.   *E.W. Fry*

was abolished and all down trains were booked to stop at Northam for ticket examination.

By the early 1870s the amount of goods traffic being dealt with was such that it was necessary for additional accommodation to be made available, so in 1876 the Rail-

way Company acquired a portion of the meadows adjoining the Deanery grounds. On this site a small engine depot was established, and this enabled the engine shed adjoining the goods shed in Canute Road to be utilised for goods traffic.

The two level crossings were a continual source of complaint, particularly at Bridge Road, where it was necessary to close the gates to the public for every shunt movement in and out of the station, in addition to the normal train service. The anomaly of this was that the level crossing could have been abolished in the early 1860s for when the Railway Company applied for permission to provide additional sidings over the crossing the Board of Trade were in favour of stipulating the provision of a bridge, but they were then not supported by the Council.

In 1872 the LSWR sought powers to acquire land in the area to improve their facilities, and in addition it was proposed to close both level crossings and provide one road overbridge. The Council wanted two bridges erected and the matter developed into a long, drawn out controversy. The gates at both these crossings fenced the railway when closed, but when they were open to road traffic, owing to the number of lines involved, they did not entirely fence the road.

In 1876 a census was taken for six days at both level crossings when it was revealed that during the six days 6,839 train movements were made over Bridge Road crossing and the gates were closed for a total of 5 days 19 hours and 18 minutes out of a total of six days. The total number

GWR 4-4-0 No. 1126 (formerly M. & S.W.J.R. No. 8) with a through train from Cheltenham approaches Southampton Terminus about 1935. The locomotive was withdrawn from service in 1938. In the background is the footbridge linking Marsh Lane with Chantry Road – the site of the level crossing until 1882. The footbridge remains today. *C.R.L. Coles*

of vehicles using the crossing during the period were 694. At Marsh Lane crossing the figures were not quite so bad, there were 2,388 train movements and the gates were closed for a total of 3 days 8 hours and 13 minutes. The number of vehicles using the crossing being 2,274.

Final agreement was reached in 1879, and the Railway Company obtained powers under an 1880 Act to construct the present Central bridge – 272 feet in length with its double road approach on the western end, one road leading from Bridge Road and the other from Marsh Lane. The footbridge at Marsh Lane was retained and remains in use today, although it was extended over additional railway lines. The construction of the Central bridge was carried out by the local firm of J. Bull & Sons at the cost of £50,000, and the bridge was opened to the public on 28th July 1882. An iron plate recording the names of those connected with the work still exists on the bridge, which now forms the western approach to the River Itchen bridge opened in 1977. It is interesting to note that the name of James Lemon, who was the Engineer for Southampton Corporation at the time does not appear on the sign. In his book "Reminiscences of Public Life in Southampton", Sir James Lemon refers to this omission as follows :– "There is an iron tablet on the centre of the bridge upon which is recorded the names of those connected with it, but my name, as Engineer, is omitted – a piece of professional discourtesy to which I am indebted to the late Mr. Jacomb, the Company's Engineer".

Following the completion of the bridge five additional sidings were provided on the east side of the railway, and St. Lawrence Road was closed as a through road. This enabled the large goods shed to be constructed and this shed still remains.

Major improvements were carried out to the station layout during the early part of 1891, when three additional platform lines were brought into use together with an additional island platform on the town side of the existing platforms. Initially the new platform was called an 'Excursion' platform, and was not covered until 1906 by which time a canopy had been erected. As a result of the goods traffic being transferred to the St. Lawrence road side of the station it was possible to redesign the station yard – five sidings being provided in 1891 to deal with parcels traffic by passenger trains. A new signal box, to become known as Southampton Yard, was also brought into use at the London end of the platforms. This box was the largest in the Southampton area being fitted with a 101 lever frame. In December 1902 a platform route indicator was fitted to the down home signal and this enabled the number of home signals to be reduced from seven to one.

The signal box at Chapel level crossing was originally on the down side of the line north of the level crossing. This box being very high and partly overhung the down goods line. In May 1889 a new signal box was constructed on the upside of the line on the Terminus station side, being fitted with a 31 lever frame.

At one time during the early part of this century a footbridge existed at the London end of platforms Nos. 2/3 (these were renumbered Nos. 4/5 in 1928).

During 1924 various comparatively minor improvements were made to the layout, but the most noticeable of these occurred in July 1924, when two of the platform lines

Above: Southampton Terminus Motive Power Sub-Depot in 1948. A somewhat primitive depot, but used mainly for re-fuelling. The locomotive being coaled was the station pilot – 02 class No. S182 – with 'British Railways' on the tanks and the temporary 'S' prefix to the number. In the background behind the wall is Deanery School. *Eric Small*

Right: Another view of the Motive Power Depot at Southampton Terminus with 'B4' No. 30096 shunting vans.
G. Bixley collection

and the carriage siding between them, all of which extended to the South Western Hotel were reduced by 45 yards, and this enabled the private roadway to be constructed between the hotel and the station concourse. At the end of 1927 an overall glass roof was erected over the roadway covering the hotel entrance and the station concourse. This roadway now serves as the main entrance to South Western House.

A new parcels office was brought into use during 1926, and two years later the six platforms were renumbered in the reverse order, starting with No.1 on the west side instead of the east side of the station.

At one time many through carriage workings operated to and from the Terminus – the *Railway Magazine* of December 1905 mentioned that in addition to the normal services provided by the LSWR, the Didcot, Newbury & Southampton Railway (worked by the GWR) and the Midland & South Western Junction Railway, many coaches belonging to other railway companies could be regularly seen including the GWR, Caledonian, Great Northern, Great Central, Midland and Furness. No doubt many of these were in connection with steamer movements, as were the through carriages which left Aberdeen and Glasgow on Thursday nights in the 1920s.

The through services operated from Didcot, Newbury and via the M. & S.W. Junction lasted into British Railway days, but the principal services to and from London were

Above: Southampton Terminus station looking rather empty, taken from No. 3 platform showing Southampton Yard box and the Central Bridge.

Author's collection

Below: Southampton Terminus – platforms 5/6 taken from No. 4 platform and looking towards the buffer stops.

Roger Hardingham collection

Above: Air raid damage which occurred to Southampton Terminus station and South Western Hotel on 23rd November 1940 and in the foreground the damaged Canute Road Crossing box can be seen. This photograph taken soon after the damage occurred shows a freight train passing across Canute Road into the Old (Eastern) Docks, while the Signal & Telegraph staff are up the pole endeavouring to restore the telephone service.

Associated British Ports courtesy Southampton City Museums

Right: Southampton Yard Box – located at the London end of Nos. 3/4 platforms at Southampton Terminus – the largest signal box in the Southampton area. It was taken out of use in December 1970.   *Robert Humm collection*

gradually concentrated on Southampton West with the through workings to and from Bournemouth, and the Terminus was finally used for local services covering Reading, Alton and Portsmouth.

For many years a large number of vans of fish, often as many as twenty a day, from various stations, in particular Aberdeen, Hull and Grimsby, were dealt with in the station yard at the Terminus, but this traffic finally ceased in the early 1960s.

All "smalls" goods traffic for the Southampton area was dealt with through the Large Goods Shed in St. Lawrence Road opposite the Terminus station for many

years, but with the decline of such traffic the Shed was eventually taken over by Pickford Haulage. In spring of 1990 they vacated the premises and a planning application has been made to convert the building into offices.

During the Second World War Southampton Terminus had its fair share of damage during various air raids on the town. There was a demand for a staff canteen and this was provided near Canute Road, being opened by Mr. R.M.T. Richards, then Traffic Manager on the 30th November 1943.

In September 1952 a new 82 lever frame was installed in Southampton Yard box. The Hampshire diesel–electric

Above: The forecourt of Southampton Terminus station on a wet day in February 1950. Horse drawn delivery vans can be seen in the parcels yard. There were then still three or four horse drawn vehicles carrying out daily deliveries in the vicinity of the station. They were replaced by motor vehicles later in the 1950s.

Left: The concourse at Southampton Terminus in the 1950s showing W.H. Smith's bookstall which was located at the rear of the buffer stops of No. 4 and 5 platform lines.

Both author's collection

Another view of the concourse at Southampton Terminus showing the entrance to Nos. 3/4 platforms and the Train Indicator Board.
Roger Hardingham collection

units appeared on the scene in 1957 and they took over the local services from Southampton Terminus, particularly to Reading and Alton. As late as 1965 an average of 85 trains per day were operating in and out of the station, but the number of passengers involved had considerably declined.

With the electrification of the main line to Bournemouth the decision was made to close the station and at the TUCC enquiry held in November 1965 concerning the proposal, there were very few objections. It was revealed that only an average of 1530 passengers were using the station each day. Southampton Terminus was officially closed to passenger traffic as from Monday 5th September 1966, the last day of service being Saturday 3rd September. After the closure the station was used for Christmas mails and parcels traffic in 1966 and again in 1967, and remained in use for the latter case until March 1968, during which time improved parcel handling facilities were provided at Southampton Central.

The up and down local lines between Southampton Junction and Southampton Terminus were removed in December 1968. The Yard signal box was closed on 13th December 1970, and was completely demolished in May 1971. Chapel Crossing was converted to an open type of level crossing with flashing warning lights on 11th October 1981, and the signal box was subsequently demolished.

After closure of the station the platforms were utilised for car parking by various tenants in South Western House, and after the permanent way was removed in 1971 the spaces between the platforms were filled in and taken over for car parking. The canopies over the platforms were eventually removed, and part of the platform area has now been allocated for car parking for tenants of South Western House, but the rest of the area has been developed for good quality housing. In 1966, the original 1840 building was listed as of special architectural and historic interest, and after being idle for nearly twenty years the building was completely renovated and re-opened on 12th March 1987 as Jeeves night club, being converted two years later to Curzon Casino, and is now Stanley Casino.

Above: Southampton Terminus – 26th June 1957 – two standard class locomotives – No. 76012 departs with a train and No. 76064 waits at platform No. 6.
R.C. Riley

Below: M7 class No. 30376 acting as Station Pilot shunting coaches from No. 6 platform at Southampton Terminus on 25th June 1957. The two lines to the left of No. 6 platform served the Old (Eastern) Docks – one of these two lines is now the sole railway link with those Docks. In the background, two Cunard Line's ships are in the Docks, the three funnelled *Queen Mary* at the Ocean Terminal and the *Saxonia*.
R.C. Riley

Above: Drummond's 'T9' No. 30707 with a van train approaches Southampton Terminus in November 1960. The large Southampton Yard signal box can be seen partly hidden by the Central bridge on which is a Southampton Corporation Transport Guy Arab on its way to the city centre having just left the Floating Bridge hard. *P.J. Cupper*

Below: The 16.53 Southampton Terminus worked by 'U' class No. 31639 leaves platform No. 2 on 24th July 1962, while No. 30497 waits with another train at platform No. 5. In the background is the large Goods Shed completed in the late 1880s. *E.W. Fry*

Above: Inside Southampton Goods Shed on 29th June 1950 – looking out towards the entrance. *Author's collection*
Below: The unsheeting deck in Southampton Goods Shed on the same day. *Author's collection*

SOUTHAMPTON DOCKS STATION –
the LSWR terminus in 1870

Ticket Platform

To Floating Bridge

Bridge Road

Terminus Terrace

Oxford Street

St. Lawrence Road

Imperial Hotel

To Town Quay

Canute Road

Southampton Docks

Drawn by
Amanda Yektaparast

Above: Rebuilt Merchant Navy class No. 35017 *Belgian Marine* passes Southampton Tunnel Junction signal box with the 08.53 Bournemouth Central to Waterloo on Sunday 13th September 1964. *M.J. Fox*

Right: A Midland & South Western Junction Railway train about 1900 on the Southampton Junction–Tunnel Junction side of the Northam triangle, running from Southampton Terminus to Southampton West. The locomotive, No. 18, was a 4-4-4T and the leading coach was purchased by the M. & S.W.J. Company in 1898.

Courtesy D. Bartholomew

Hampshire D.M.U. No. 1118 forming the 11.42 Salisbury–Portsmouth approaching Tunnel Junction signal box on 26th May 1963, and passing the fine LSWR signals with the lower duplicate arms then still in use. The left hand distant signal was operated by Northam Junction, while the right hand one was worked from Southampton Junction Box.

M.J. Fox

Above: Clearing up after an air raid on 8th July 1941 – St. Marys Street bridge between Southampton Tunnel Junction and the eastern mouth of Southampton Tunnel. The buildings demolished were the National Provincial Bank and the undertakers F. & E. Beeston. The Brickwoods pub was the Bridge Tavern, and the building remains today, now the Bridge Gallery. While the lines were blocked trains from Waterloo to Bournemouth travelled via the Docks and those from Bournemouth to Waterloo passed via Romsey and Chandlers Ford. *Author's collection*

Left: The other end of Southampton Tunnel – the eastern end which does not very often appear in photographs. This picture was taken in March 1965 when repairs were being carried out to Southampton Tunnel and single line working was in operation over the 'down' line. *Bert Moody*

King Arthur class No. 787 *Sir Menadeuke*, one of the class built at the North British Locomotive Works at Glasgow, emerges from Southampton Tunnel on 8th July 1929, on the 16.30 Waterloo to Bournemouth – 'The Bournemouth Limited', on the first day that this train entered service. The engine was completed in 1925 and was based at Bournemouth until 1937, when it was transferred to Exmouth Junction Depot. The 'Bournemouth Limited', which was originally advertised as 'a corridor and restaurant car express' was booked to run each week day non-stop between Bournemouth Central and Waterloo, leaving Bournemouth Central at 08.40 and returning from Waterloo at 16.30, covering the 108 miles in two hours. The set number of the leading coach can be seen – No. 431 which in 1929 was a three coach set formed of 3rd corridor brake 3181, first class corridor 7170 and 3rd corridor brake 3182, all LSWR 57' Ironclad stock built in 1921 as LSWR five coach set No. 1C, and reduced to a three set in 1929 for the Bournemouth Limited. About 1931 it was made a four coach set with the addition of 3rd class coach 717. The 'Bournemouth Limited' was withdrawn after the outbreak of War in September 1939 and never reinstated. In 1951 two trains running in somewhat similar timings – 07.38 Weymouth to Waterloo and the 16.35 Waterloo to Weymouth were given the name *Royal Wessex*, but both these trains were booked to stop at Southampton Central.

Author's collection

Blechynden and Southampton West

Sections 33 and 34 of the Act authorising the construction of Southampton & Dorchester Railway read as follows:–

33. And it be enacted that the Company shall before the opening of the Railway for public use, make at such points on or near the shore of Southampton Water and near the eastern end of Blechynden Terrace as shall be agreed on between the Company and the said Mayor, Alderman and Burgesses and afterwards maintain, a station, with all such houses, warehouses, offices, yards, apparatus and other works and conveniences as the Engineer of the said company shall consider requisite for the

It would seem from the wording of Section 33 that a station on a grander style would be erected, but this eventually proved completely the opposite, in fact it looked at one time as though there would be no station at all at Blechynden. Work did start on the construction of a station near the tunnel mouth, partly on land known as King John's Pond and partly on adjoining land owned by Southampton Corporation, but the work was stopped. Official notice was given that the line would be opened for traffic on 1st June 1847, but there was still no firm indication that the Railway Company intended to provide a station at Blechynden, so the Town Council quickly took action to stop the opening

The scene of the 'down' side of the line looking back towards the town in about 1890. Some of this area of water was later reclaimed to enable the Corporation's Electricity Generating station to be erected in 1902/3. The church on the skyline is Kingsfields Congregational church then situated in Havelock Road. The church was closed in the early 1900s and after standing idle for several years was adapted for use as a Labour Exchange. It was eventually demolished to enable the roadway to be constructed in 1936 from Civic Centre Road to the Western Esplanade. *Author's collection*

proper accommodation of the public and that adequate provision shall be made by the stoppage of a sufficient number of trains per diem for the purpose of taking up and setting down passengers and goods at the said station.

34. Construct and maintain for two years a public walk on the southern or south western side of such part of the railway as shall be made on the shore and mudlands of Southampton Water.

of the line until Section 33 was complied with. As a result a "temporary station for the accommodation of the public was provided" – in fact the premises known as Ivy House in Blechynden Terrace and owned by Mr. Purkis were leased for use as the station offices.

A level crossing was provided west of the station platforms giving access to the water front.

The use of Mr. Purkis' house continued until 1850,

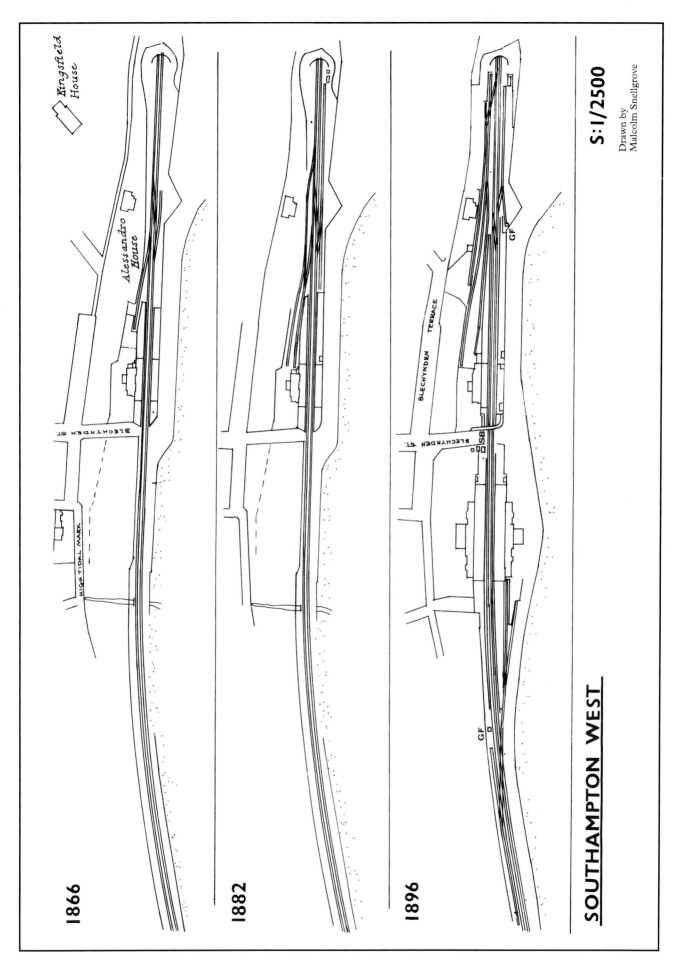

1866

1882

1896

SOUTHAMPTON WEST

S:1/2500

Drawn by
Malcolm Snellgrove

59

Above: In the early 1890s a Bournemouth West to Eastleigh train approaches Southampton West station. The signal box is on the right of the photograph. The land behind the fence is where the new Southampton West station was erected in 1894/5. In the background is Four Post Hill. The wooden signal post is of interest particularly the old type of slotted signal at the top.

The late D. Pye's collection

Left: 'N15' class No. 743 *Lyonesse* passes the out of use original Southampton West (formerly Blechynden) station with a 'down' train of GWR coaches in the late 1920s. The building on the left was adapted for use as a Goods Office/ Shed and remained in use as such for many years. *L. & G.R.P.*

Lord Kitchener returned from South Africa on 12th July 1902, and here is the special train which conveyed him to Paddington station. The train is standing in the 'up' siding at the Millbrook end of Southampton West station and was booked to leave at 10.45. Drummond 'T9' No. 773 (renumbered 733 in 1924) is suitably decorated while the rolling stock was then the latest on the LSWR, the fourth vehicle is a saloon. 773 worked the train to Basingstoke, where it was replaced by GWR 3374 *Baden Powell* which had been renamed 'Kitchener' for the occasion which took the train on to Paddington.

C.H. Eden

61

Two views of the 'up' platform at South-ampton West station taken from the 'down' platform in 1911. The arched brickwork on concrete foundations supporting the plat-forms can be clearly seen, and these arches can still be seen today on the Northam end of Nos. 1 and 2 platforms.

Both author's collection

when it would seem that a building which had been pre-pared for use at Cosham station, but not used in view of the joint arrangements made with the London, Brighton & South Coast Railway, was utilised at Blechynden.

In 1858 plans were prepared for an enlarged station and from deposited plans the approximate length of the platforms of the original station was sixty feet (sufficient to accommodate three to four carriages of the period). Despite the limited facilities provided, gas lighting had been in-stalled for at a meeting of the LSWR Land Ways & Works

Committee on 29th September 1848, a bill for £35 for the rent of gas fittings at Blechynden was produced and in-structions given to purchase the gas fittings on a five year purchase, instead of paying rent.

At the end of July 1858 the LSWR published an official announcement to the effect that as from Monday 2nd August Blechynden station would be called Southampton West or West End station.

In October 1859 plans for enlarging the station at a cost of £5,000 were agreed and the contract was awarded

Southampton West – the level crossing and signal box. The level crossing was closed in 1934 when the road overbridge at the Millbrook end of the station was opened. The signal box remained in use for another year when the new signal box at the west end of the station was brought into use.   *Author's collection*

to Mr. Bull, a local builder. The work was completed towards the end of 1860. The accommodation then available consisted of a booking office and two waiting rooms on the up (to London) platform and two small waiting rooms on the down platform. It is interesting to mention here that a portion of the upside station building existed until the 1950s, being used as a goods office and store for many years.

In 1866 the level crossing gates and various points were operated by hand by staff. The majority of level crossings were a source of complaint and the one at Southampton West was no exception. The *Southampton Times* of 10th February 1872 contained a report on the level crossing which read as follows:– "some alterations have recently been made to the gates of the railway crossing at Blechynden with a view both to regulate the traffic on the line and to hold in check that which may be passing over it. The large gates have been fitted with central signals, so that the drivers of approaching trains can easily perceive when they are not thrown back. At the same time the side gates for foot passengers have been made to fasten by a new contrivance, which keeps them effectively closed while the large gates are shut, and as a consequence there is no chance of passing over the line when trains are either at or near the station. Occasionally this is of considerable duration and numbers of vehicles and foot passengers are frequently to be seen waiting on either side. Level crossings must always be objectionable and in a town like Southampton with its increasing traffic ought to be unknown, but the public are entitled to have them regulated with a due regard to their convenience and this is in no way second in importance to the plea of public safety".

In 1885 a footbridge was provided at the level crossing, and this remains in use today, the brick supports on the upside of the line being part of the original structure. It

would seem that the side or wicket gates at the level crossing were removed, when the footbridge was erected. The original signal box at Southampton West was located on the upside adjacent to the level crossing on the Millbrook side and this structure was also fitted with the large roof ventilator. In 1896 there were 24 levers in the signal box. In addition there were two ground frames at Southampton West – Ground Frame 'A' near the Tunnel mouth had a 16 lever frame and Ground Frame 'B' at the west end being equipped with a 19 lever frame.

The LSWR acquired in 1887 the premises known as 'Alessandro' in Kingsbridge Lane, and this 1842 building was first used as the Station Master's residence, and later for other railway purposes. It was eventually demolished in November 1975.

By the end of the 1880s the station was completely inadequate for the needs of the public, and consideration was given to the construction of a more centrally situated station, but it was eventually decided to provide this on the western side of the level crossing. Early in the 1890s Southampton Corporation sold an area of land to the LSWR for £3,500 for the construction of the new station. The land involved was partly field and partly shoreline and was therefore subject to tidal flooding. As a result it was necessary for massive foundations, about thirty feet deep, to be built, particularly on the downside where the original shoreline dropped away. Arched brickwork between concrete foundations supported the platforms and this can still be seen today on certain parts of Nos. 1 and 2 platfroms.

The new station was brought into use on 1st November 1895 without any ceremony and it was then claimed that the station was one of the best and most commodious on the London & South Western Railway. The most notable feature was the clock tower on the upside, 82 feet high with a cupola top. The up platform had a length of 600 feet,

while the down platform was 800 feet in length. The down bay platform provided at the Bournemouth end of the station was 500 feet. At the London end of the platforms a covered footbridge of cast iron with glazed windows was erected, while on the down platform a building was provided with footwarming apparatus, and this was capable of heating 49 footwarmers at one time. With the introduction of steam heating of trains the equipment was no longer required and the room was converted to a coal store in 1912. In 1895 over sixty passenger trains per day were stopping at the station.

Southampton Corporation built their electricity generating station on reclaimed land not far from the station on the downside of the line and the station was brought into use in 1904. To enable coal to be supplied to the generating station a siding was constructed connecting with the down line just west of the tunnel mouth, being worked by electric locomotives owned by the Corporation. In February 1907 the LSWR agreed to take electricity for lighting and power for the West station.

Early in 1910 the down platform and bay platform were lengthened by about 100 feet at the west end and the connection to the bay line moved westward accordingly. The next development took place during 1912/13 when a building was constructed at the western end of the upside forecourt for accommodating the Central Divisional Manager and his staff who were then located in Eastleigh. In April 1917 a connection was made from the Down Bay siding for the Train Ferry jetty being constructed near the Royal Pier.

The Southampton Docks & Marine Sports Club was opened in November 1922 at the West station by Major G.S. Szlumper, then Docks & Marine Manager. The building was originally occupied by the YMCA during the First World War and was located at the eastern end of the upside forecourt. The building was replaced by new premises on the same site in 1937.

During the early 1920s nearly three million passengers were using the station each year. In addition 97,000 parcels were dealt with annually while about 1,000 milk churns

Right: Southampton West station in December 1931 with the construction of the New (Western) Docks in progress in the background. The level crossing can be clearly seen, but the signal box is hidden by the water tower. In those days the station consisted of two main platforms, one for 'up' trains and one for 'down' trains, with a short bay on the 'down' side at the Millbrook end. During the First World War it was from this bay line that the connection was made to the Train Ferry Jetty situated up river from the Royal Pier, and the remains of that line can be seen in the picture immediately behind the row of taxis in the 'down' side forecourt. The water tower remained until the end of steam traction in 1967, and the Clock Tower together with the 'up' side

buildings were demolished in 1966. The brick building in the 'up' side yard close to the road leading to the level crossing was the Docks & Marine Sports & Social Club, which was destroyed during the War. The 'down' side buildings were replaced in the middle 1930s when additional running lines were constructed. *Southern Evening Echo*

Right: The 'down' platform at Southampton West in 1929 with a chalk train from Micheldever being propelled on to the remaining portion of the old train ferry line. The chalk was being used for the reclamation of land in connection with the construction of the New (Western) Docks. *Author's collection*
Below: If the tide was exceptionally high the 'down' side station yard was often flooded – in fact occasionally the railway tracks were also flooded as seen in the photograph below taken in November 1924. *Mrs A.M. Weller*

Above: The reconstruction of Southampton West station in July 1934 – the shuttering is in position for the station footbridge and lift, both remain in use today. In the background can be seen the Empire Theatre (now The Mayflower) and the then newly completed Civic Centre. *Below:* The start of the reconstruction of Southampton West station in 1933/4 – a steam crane is unloading rail on to the 'down' platform from wagons stood on the 'down' bay line. The 'down' platform was rebuilt to form the Island platform of today. *Author's collection*

The road overbridge at the Millbrook end of Southampton station taken in 1934 after being opened to the public, which enabled the level crossing to be closed. The station reconstruction of the 'down' side is in progress and reclamation of the land for the New (Western) Docks is continuing. Wagons on a temporary railway track can be seen at the far end of the bridge.

Associated British Ports courtesy Southampton City Museums

were handled each week. It was revealed in 1923 that the number of times that the level crossing gates were operated during a normal 24 hours was 292 times, and delays to road traffic were increasing. Suggestions were made with a view to the abolition of the crossing, but this did not take place until 25th June 1934, following the construction of the road overbridge at the west end of the station.

In 1926 the offices of the Divisional Superintendent (formerly Manager) were enlarged and a new parcels office was erected at the west end of the upside station buildings. The ground frame at the west end of the station was moved about 100 yards nearer Millbrook in May 1927, and this enabled the up platform to be lengthened by 300 feet, giving a total length of 900 feet.

In connection with the development of the New Docks (Western Docks of today) two additional running lines were to be provided between Millbrook and Southampton West, and at the same time the facilities at the latter station were to be improved with the provision of two additional platform lines. The work was commenced in 1933 and the original down line eventually became the up through line, serving the present No. 2 platform. The down platform (No. 4) was constructed to serve the new down local line and the new bay line. Following closure of the level crossing a new signal box was built on the upside at the west end of the station. This box was fitted with a 75 lever Westinghouse frame and was brought into use on 2nd June 1935, together with the new layout.

On 7th July 1935 Southampton West was renamed Southampton Central.

Southampton West Goods Yard looking towards the Tunnel, taken early in 1935. The signal box (lower foreground) remains but the crossing has been removed to enable the additional lines on the 'down' side to be laid in. In the foreground behind the signal box was the Docks & Marine Sports Club which was rebuilt in 1937 and destroyed in the bombing of the 1940s. The remains of the original Southampton West (formerly Blechynden) station, then in use as a Goods Shed/Office, can be seen immediately behind the water tower. The large warehouse on the left was destroyed during the bombing, although parts of the walls of the cellars can still be seen today in the small garden which now exists. It will be noted that there is no roadway on the 'down' side from the Civic Centre – this was not commenced until 1936.

Author's collection

Southampton Central

In June 1935 new station buildings were brought into use on the downside of the station, and thus began the long era which still exists today, where the style of the buildings on one side of the station is completely different from that on the other side. The new buildings were constructed in the concrete style of the Southern Railway of the 1930s, and the accommodation comprised a spacious ticket hall, ticket office and small enquiry office, refreshment room with staff accommodation above, waiting room, foreman's office, toilets and a large parcels and left luggage office. In the ticket hall a large attractive display panel showed a map of Southampton Docks and gave details of shipping movements.

Above: The new 'down' side entrance to Southampton Central in 1935 – typical of the type of building then being constructed by the Southern Railway. Unfortunately this building had a very short life for it was completely destroyed when struck by a German parachute mine in July 1941. *Author's collection*

Below: The booking hall on the 'down' side at Southampton Central was very spacious, this picture, taken in 1936, shows the large board provided near the entrance to the platforms giving the position of vessels in Southampton Docks, including arrivals and sailings. At 44 berth the name of Cunard White Star liner *Queen Mary* is shown – 1936 was the year that the liner entered service. On the left is a large platform ticket machine, while through the open gateway the then new island platform can be seen. The booking hall was completely destroyed during the early hours of 22nd July 1941. *Author's collection*

Above: Southampton Central – the Refreshment Room in the new 'down' side buildings in 1936.   *Author's collection*

Left: The damaged 'up' side buildings at Southampton Central as a result of an air raid on 23rd November 1940. The building on the left was the Docks & Marine Sports Club destroyed in a later air raid.   *Author's collection*

Above: During the early hours of 22nd July 1941 two parachute mines were dropped on to the station. This photograph shows the damage caused to the Island platform.   *Author's collection*

Below: The damaged No. 4 platform buildings – the ticket hall being destroyed completely.   *Author's collection*

Left: The destroyed 'down' side buildings after the parachute mines had hit the buildings. 22nd July 1941.
Author's collection
Below: Southampton Central – Watering engine No. 35014 *Nederland Line* on the 'down' Bournemouth Belle on 12th May 1949. *D.P.N. Callender*

In May 1936 work commenced on the provision of a new roadway leading from Civic Centre Road to the downside of the station, and on 30th July 1936 loudspeakers were used on the station for the first time.

By October 1938 all parcels traffic for collection or delivery by railway cartage vehicles was being dealt with at Southampton Terminus, but there was still a considerable quantity of "carted by public" traffic passing through Southampton Central.

Shortly after the outbreak of World War Two a train control office for the Southern District was constructed on the upside near the mouth of Southampton Tunnel in a concrete bunker at ground level. The office was usually damp and often quite wet. In those days the Southern District office was responsible for the area covering Dorchester, Salisbury and Cosham. This control office remained in use until July 1953, by which time the District Traffic Superintendent's office, in the forecourt on the upside of the Central station, had been enlarged to enable the control to be transferred to that building.

Unfortunately the main part of the station building on the downside had an extremely short life for it was badly damaged when three parachute mines fell in the vicinity during the early hours of 22nd June 1941, killing one member of the staff and causing considerable damage to the whole station. All the lines were out of use for some

Above: Lord Nelson class No. 30858 *Lord Duncan* on 'down' Waterloo to Bournemouth train leaving No. 4 platform at Southampton Central on 19th April 1952.   *L. Elsey*
Below: Drummond's 'M7' No. 30375 0-4-4T on 'up' local train to Eastleigh leaving Southampton Central.   *Roger Hardingham collection*

Schools class No. 30902 *Wellington* leaving Southampton Central on the 11.43 Saturdays only Lymington Pier to Waterloo, on 25th August 1962. The then new telephone exchange is behind the locomotive. *M.J. Fox*

hours. Emergency repairs were subsequently carried out to the parts of the building which were still usable, and they have remained in use until the present day, the destroyed central section being replaced by a modern glass fronted structure in 1980.

Passenger traffic through the Central remained at a very high level, for example in 1958 the number of tickets collected exceeded 1,336,300, while the number of tickets issued reached 732,770. In addition more than 106,000 parcels and items of passengers luggage in advance were dealt with in that year.

It was regular practice for through coaches for the Docks on ordinary services to be detached at Southampton Central and worked specially into the Docks, when the number of passengers involved did not justify the running of a special boat train.

In March 1963 a new telephone exchange was opened on top of the wartime control office – this exchange covered the area from Winchester to Weymouth and replaced the railway omnibus telephone network which was introduced in 1923.

In September 1963 much of the work performed in the District Manager's office was transferred to the Divisional Manager's office at Wimbledon, but the building remained in use for various railway purposes, including the train control, for several years later, being finally demolished early in 1971 in order to improve the road access to the new upside buildings.

In June 1966, owing to the then pending closure of Southampton Terminus station, all parcels traffic for delivery and collection by railway cartage vehicles in the Southampton area was transferred to the Central station. As a result various alterations were made to the parcels office and loading dock adjoining No. 5 platform (Down Bay) line in order to provide a larger circulating area for BRUT trollies, then in use, and for dealing with additional Post Office mails, in particular the Up and Down Travelling

Post Office mail trains which had always been dealt with at Southampton Terminus.

It was announced in 1965 that a new four storey building would be erected on the upside, allowing for office accommodation to be available above the station facilities on the ground floor. The demolition of the 1895 building, including the clock tower, was commenced in August 1966 and the subsequent construction of the new building caused considerable inconvenience to both passengers and staff. The resultant new building, part of which was brought into use in October 1967, provided very limited accommodation for passengers and staff – thus an excellent opportunity was lost to provide a station worthy of the City of Southampton.

With the introduction of the full electric train service on 10th July 1967, the word 'Central' was dropped from the title of the station, although it remained on the signal box, until the box was closed on 8th November 1981, with the introduction of track circuit block working controlled from Eastleigh Box. All the lines through the station were then signalled for reversible working as were the two lines through Southampton Tunnel, i.e., trains can now run in either direction over these lines. At the same time the designation of the running lines between Southampton and Millbrook was altered, the Through lines became the Slow lines and the Local lines became the Fast lines.

The footbridge at the London end of the station at the site of the former level crossing was renovated in 1987 and now carries a row of painted shipping international code flags which reads 'Welcome to Southampton'. Later in the same year major renovations were commenced at the station and in 1988 a much improved booking hall/ticket office and enquiry office were brought into use on the upside, together with a new buffet and bookstall. At the same time various minor alterations were made to the downside buildings and a modern 140 foot ceramic mosaic, claimed to depict images of the City's past, present and future was unveiled on the station footbridge.

Above: 'N' class No. 31852 2-6-0 leaving Southampton Central with a Salisbury to Portsmouth & Southsea train in the early 1950s.
Pursey C. Short

Below: An 'up' train worked by a Lord Nelson class locomotive approaches Southampton Central on the 'up' through line from Millbrook pass the signal box built in 1935, on 23rd June 1955.
D.H. Cull

Left: The 'Bournemouth Belle' with No. 35018 *British India* in May 1956 gets away from Southampton Central under the signal gantry, while No. 30851 *Sir Francis Drake* waits in the Bay Road. No. 35018 is now preserved on the Mid Hants Railway.

Author's collection

Below: British Railways Standard Pacific No. 70009 *Alfred The Great*, with the 'Bournemouth Belle' leaving Southampton Central in 1951. Millbrook have not yet cleared the line to Redbridge as the 'down' local outer distant signal is still in the 'on' position.

The late G. Wheeler

Above: Rebuilt Battle of Britain class No. 34053 *Sir Keith Park* on a Waterloo to Weymouth train emerges from Southampton Tunnel on 23rd June 1962. Immediately behind the engine is the Telephone Exchange. In the foreground the track leading to the Electricity Generating Station still remain – it was finally removed in April 1964.   *M.J. Fox*

Below: Battle of Britain class No. 34109 *Sir Trafford Leigh-Mallory* stands in No. 1 platform letting off steam with a Bristol–Portsmouth & Southsea train on 20th April 1952.   *L. Elsey*

Left: West Country class No. 34008 *Padstow* working on Special Conducted Rambler Jubilee Excursion passing through Southampton Central on Easter Sunday 21st April 1957. The train ran from Waterloo to Dorchester and Upwey via Ringwood.

Author's collection

Left: Freight engine class 'Q' No. 33007 works on a troop train formed of Eastern Region stock through Southampton on 19th July 1958.   *E.W. Fry*

Below: The 'Bournemouth Belle' with No. 35015 *Rotterdam Lloyd* leaving Southampton Central 17th September 1949. An unidentified Lord Nelson class stands in No. 5 Bay Platform.   *S.W. Baker*

Above: Ex GWR 'Manor' class No. 7808 *Cookham Manor* leaves Southampton Central with a through train to Cheltenham on 15th September 1956.   *E.W. Fry*
Below: No. 3212 with a local train of non-corridor Southern stock leaving Southampton Central on 27th August 1955.   *L. Elsey*

Above: Merchant Navy class No. 35028 *Clan Line* leaving Southampton Central with Waterloo to Bournemouth train on 10th September 1949. The nameplates are boarded up prior to being officially named. *Pursey C. Short*
Below: Eighteen years later, on 25th March 1967, the same locomotive departs at 1405 with the 'Bournemouth Belle'. It was a rare sight at this stage in the electrification process as the 'Belle' was usually diesel hauled from December 1966. *Roger Hardingham*

Above: For many years the Southern Railway and later the Southern Region of British Railways has created interest among the station staff in maintaining stations clean and tidy by holding 'Best Kept Station' competitions. This photograph taken in November 1981 shows some of the awards being presented. For in that year in Group 'B' for larger stations, Southampton were the winners, while Group 'C' St. Denys were first, and in Group 'C' (for the Eastleigh area) Romsey were first. In the photograph are Senior Railman Fred Eastman and Station Manager Richard Newman (both of St. Denys), Mr. Bernard Whitehall (South-West Divisional Manager), Railman Philip Wyre (Southampton) Mr. C.G. Earl (Area Manager), Station Manager Sid Everett (Southampton), Leading Railman Maurice Eldridge and Station Manager John Spiers (both of Romsey).   *Hampshire Chronicle*

Right: A special train conveying a 124 transformer for the then new power station at Marchwood on 22nd January 1956. The train was worked specially on the 'up' and 'up' local lines from Northam to Millbrook to ensure sufficient clearance for the abnormal load through Southampton Tunnel.
      D.H. Cull

Above and left: The District Office located in the 'up' side station forecourt at Southampton West, was opened in 1913, and remained in use until 1971 when the building was demolished. The above photographs were taken in the late 1960s. Over the years the officer in charge held various titles, varying from District Goods Manager to District Traffic Superintendent. It ceased to operate as an Area Office in 1963 when it was merged, together with the office at Woking, to form the South Western Divisional Manager's office at Wimbledon, but the building remained in use for various railway purposes, including the District Control office which was located in the extension which was added in 1953 and part of this extension can be seen on the right of the picture on the left. *The late D.S. Hunt*

Left: Inside the wartime built Control Office for the Southern District in 1953. The office was in a concrete bunker at ground level near the mouth of Southampton Tunnel. Shortly after the photograph was taken the office was transferred to the extension which had been constructed on to the District Office in the forecourt of Southampton Central station.
G.A. Jacobs

Above: Empty tank wagons on the way to Fawley passes through Southampton behind Urie's class H16 No. 30517 on 27th August 1960.
E.W. Fry

Below: April 1983 – Repairs to Southampton Tunnel underway again – this time the contractors, Edmund Nuttall, utilised a narrow gauge railway to convey the material into and out of the tunnel and the locomotive used can just be seen over the top of the Edmund Nuttall board. The train is a Portsmouth Harbour–Bristol train hauled by an unidentified class 33.
I.J. Bovey

Millbrook

As a result of a request from local inhabitants, the provision of a station at Millbrook was considered by the Court of Directors on 12th September 1861. It was agreed that a small station, similar to the one provided at Portswood, should be erected at Millbrook where the public road runs close to the railway, and it was decided that the work of constructing the station in wood should be commenced at once. The work must have proceeded quickly for the station was opened on 1st November 1861. During the following month it was decided to have gas lighting installed and arrangements were made for the Shirley Gas Company to provide a gas supply and to erect lamps and fittings.

in 1935 major alterations were made to the station. The down platform was rebuilt and lengthened, becoming an island platform served by the down and up through lines, the up platform being abolished. The level crossing was closed on 1st May 1935 and as a result the station footbridge was replaced by a ramped bridge, thus maintaining the right of way to the foreshore. New station buildings and a canopy were erected on the island platform and access to the station was gained via the new bridge. The ticket office was fitted with a passimeter to gain access to the platform. A new siganl box, fitted with a 70 lever Westinghouse frame, was erected between the up and down through lines at the Redbridge end of the platform and was brought into

The entrance to Millbrook station in LSWR days. The wooden building is the ticket office. The small building immediately in front of the crane is the coal order office for Holden & Sons, one of the coal merchants who operated from Millbrook goods yard.

M. Snellgrove collection

A short siding was later provided at the back of the up platform with a trailing connection from the up line at the Southampton end of the station. A signal box was erected at the level crossing which existed at the Redbridge end of the station. This crossing gave access to a small boat yard and to the foreshore.

In 1907 a long siding with a trailing connection from the up line was provided on the Redbridge side of the station, and this became the basis for the goods yard which was gradually enlarged, and by the middle of the 1920s consisted of seven sidings. In 1928 a new goods office and a large warehouse were brought into use and two additional sidings were laid in to serve the warehouse.

In conjunction with the provision of two additional running lines between Southampton Central and Millbrook

use on 2nd June 1935. Two additional lines on the dock side of the running lines were also provided giving access to and from the New (Western) Docks.

The station was unstaffed as from 22nd May 1966, and the station buildings were subsequently vandalised with the result that they were completely demolished together with the canopy in October 1968 and replaced by a small waiting shelter. Although the goods yard was still quite busy dealing with cement, coal and scrap metal traffic it was closed on 15th July 1967, and the traders were transferred to other local yards. This enabled the area to be developed at a cost of about £250,000 as a Freightliner Terminal which was opened on 29th January 1968, and remains in use today, dealing with local domestic traffic and some container traffic from the Docks. Freightliner is now part

MILBROOK STATION COUNTY SERIES 582

Above: Millbrook station looking eastwards towards Southampton from the station footbridge in the early 1920s, showing very clearly the small beach which existed at the back of the 'down' platform prior to the construction of the Western Docks.
Lens of Sutton

Right: Millbrook station looking westward prior to the 1935 alterations. The signal box can be seen at the end of the 'up' platform while behind the 'down' platform on the left can be seen part of the small yacht yard which was there for many years until the area was reclaimed for Southampton Docks.
H.J. Petterson-Rutherford

Class 'S15' No. 30507 slowing for the Millbrook stop with the 17.05 Southampton Terminus to Wimborne, and being overhauled by No. 35005 *Canadian Pacific* on the 15.20 Waterloo to Weymouth on 24th May 1963. The lines on the right are the 'from' and 'to' dock lines provided in 1935.   *M.J. Fox*

of B.R. Rail Freight Distribution sector, and since the spring of 1990, full load traffic previously dealt with at Bevois Park Sidings has been handled at Millbrook Freightliner Terminal.

With the extension of colour light signalling and track circuit block working the signal box was closed on 8th

November 1981 and subsequently demolished. At the same time the designation of the running lines between Southampton and Millbrook was altered, the Through lines became the Slow lines and the Local lines became the Fast lines.

Left: West Country No. 34093 *Saunton* with a 'down' Waterloo to Bournemouth train between Southampton Central and Millbrook. The line on the right is the end on the 'down' loop line.   *Pursey C. Short*

Above: Maunsell's 'S15' No. 30838 working a 'down' train through Millbrook. In the yard a standard 2-6-2T is carrying out shunting operations. *M.J. Fox*

Below: Southampton's first freightliner terminal under construction at Millbrook January 1968. On the 'down' line is a Portsmouth to Bristol train formed of a six car diesel unit. *Bert Moody*

Redbridge

A station was provided at Redbridge in 1847 with the opening of the Southampton & Dorchester railway. When the line was opened from Blechynden double track only existed as far as Redbridge – the remainder of the line to Dorchester via Ringwood was then single line with crossing loops at certain stations. The portion from Redbridge to Totton was doubled in August 1857. The existing station building at Redbridge on the up platform is the original and residential accommodation was provided for the station master.

On 6th March 1865 the line to Romsey was brought into use in connection with the opening of the Andover – Romsey line. Originally this line was single but the section between Romsey and Redbridge was doubled in March 1884. About the same time the passenger accommodation on the station was improved and the platforms were lengthened.

In 1880 the LSWR acquired Redbridge Wharf and adjacent land on which the Permanent Way Works was established. Access to the Works site was gained via a level crossing at the Bournemouth end of the station, where the signal box was located.

On land to the east of the original works site the firm of Dixon & Cardus, manufacturer of linseed oil and oil cake, had a Mill until it was closed at the end of the last century when the work was transferred to the Company's other premises near Northam bridge, although the Mill was not demolished until the early 1920s. Nearby there was at one time a vitriol works, which later became a chemical factory. Eventually the main creosoting plant at Redbridge Works was built on this site. Schultz Gunpowder Company established a factory on an adjacent site in 1898 and a siding

with a connection from the main line was provided. These works closed in 1922, and the connection to the siding was removed in June 1923. The site was acquired by the Southern Railway and between 1923 and 1926 major developments took place in the Permanent Way Works.

In January 1927 the position of Station Master at Redbridge was abolished and the station was placed under the control of the Station Master at Millbrook.

From about 1930 the timber firm of Bryce White & Company regularly received timber on two sidings which were parallel with the up (from Romsey) branch line – these sidings were eventually removed in September 1966.

During the early 1930s a small part of the Schultz site was utilised for an asphalt/tarmacadam works being operated by Scientific Roads (Southampton) Ltd. and a short private siding was provided with a connection from one of the sidings at the back of the down platform. After the war this depot was operated for a while by Alexander Asphalt Company Ltd.

To expedite the movement of military traffic into the New (Western) Docks new connections were brought into use on 28th March 1943 at the Millbrook end of the station – these connections were removed in February 1953.

Further developments took place at Redbridge Permanent Way Works in 1950, when the site was extended and a new foundry was built and flash–butt welding plant installed, thus making it possible for long welded rail to be produced. The Works remained fully operational until 1988 and was finally closed on 3rd March 1989.

The timber viaduct over the River Test, built when the line was opened in 1847, was replaced by an iron structure in 1883. The new viaduct being constructed just south of

Redbridge station about 1910 with an 'up' stopping train from Bournemouth to Eastleigh approaching hauled by Adams 'T6' class No. 683.
Willstead

Above: 'Hall' class No. 6924 passes through Redbridge station with an inter-regional train in 1964.

John H. Bird

Below: Redbridge station taken from the 'down' platform in September 1981.

John Scrace

the original one, and when the 1883 viaduct was replaced in 1964 the structure which exists today was built on the line of the original railway.

On the Redbridge – Romsey section a level crossing known as Test Gates existed until 18th November 1930 when the flyover was opened.

The signal box was taken out of use on 28th February 1982, but the station remains open, being served by the stopping trains between Southampton and Wareham and by certain trains running between Southampton and Salisbury.

Above: Rebuilt Merchant Navy class No. 35014 *Nederland Line* with a Bournemouth to Waterloo train approaching Redbridge station. On the left is part of the Permanent Way Works including the stone built engine shed which could accommodate just one engine.

J.R. Fairman collection
Left: One of the diesel electric multiple units, No. 1306, built for the Oxted service, formed in a SEG rail tour covering Hampshire passes Redbridge signal box on 22nd July 1978. The road access to Redbridge works can be clearly seen. *John Scrace*

Right: Sleepers being unloaded at Redbridge Wharf by
steam crane in the 1930s.   *Totton & Eling H.S.*

Right: Sleepers loaded to low trollies being pushed into the pressure
creosoting cylinders at Redbridge Works in the 1930s.
                                   Totton & Eling H.S.

Below: Redbridge Works – 12th September 1958 – a bogie wagon fitted
with small hand cranes to assist with the loading and unloading of rail.
Note the high stacks of sleepers in the background.
     Associated British Ports courtesy Southampton City Museums

Above: 'W' class 2-6-4T No. 31916 and standard class 3 2-6-2T doubleheading a tank car train from Fawley passing over the 1883 viaduct at Redbridge on 28th April 1962. *M.J. Fox*

Below: An unusual photograph taken in June 1964 showing the two viaducts at Redbridge, over the River Test. On the right, the new one brought into use at the end of May 1964, and on the left the 1883 built structure about to be removed. *E.W. Fry*

St. Denys to Netley

St. Denys from the air in the late 1920s. The line to Bitterne can be clearly seen sweeping round in a large arc before approaching the viaduct over the River Itchen.   *Author's collection*

The Southampton & Netley Railway Company was authorised to construct a railway from Portswood to Netley when Parliament passed an Act on 1st August 1861. The alignment initially provided for the junction with the LSWR to be made near St. Denys Road bridge with the connection facing from London. It was originally planned for the line to pass via the top of Lances Hill to serve Bitterne Village. Revised plans, however, were prepared and a further Act was passed on 22nd June 1863, when approximately the present alignment of the railway was agreed. Under this Act the Railway Company was empowered to enter into a traffic agreement with the LSWR. On the 14th July 1864 a further Act was passed and included therein was an alteration to the proposed junction making it facing from the Southampton direction instead of the London direction. The amalgamation of the Southampton & Netley Railway Company with the LSWR took effect from 1st January 1865.

Inspection of the new railway was carried out by the Board of Trade Inspector, Captain Tyler, on 22nd Februray 1866, and while most of the work was found to be satisfactory he reported that he was unable to agree to the line being opened as various items were not complete. The LSWR promised to give immediate attention to these

items and the line was opened to the public on 5th March 1866.

The *Southampton Times* of 3rd February 1866 gave an interesting account of the line which read as follows: "at Portswood the station is an attractive and commodious structure, everything being done to consult the comfort and convenience of passengers. On leaving the main line the railway passes over Adelaide Road by a level crossing and about a quarter of a mile beyond crosses Priory Road by a girder bridge, then over the River Itchen by an iron viaduct consisting of three 115 feet openings. Considerable difficulty was experienced in constructing the viaduct owing to the yielding nature of the bed of the river. The main girders of the bridge are supported by cast iron cylinders, which were sunk a considerable depth below the bed of the river. In some instances the foundations are bedded in concrete some 60 feet below the surface".

"About 270 tons of cast iron was used on constructing the cylinders for the piers and about 300 tons of wrought iron in the girders. The entire cost of the viaduct being about £15,000. At either end of the viaduct and over each pier are the Southampton Arms, and the bridge at night is illuminated by gas, for which four ornamental columns have been erected".

Adelaide Road crossing box on 29th January 1968 – the lifting barriers had replaced the level crossing gates in 1966. The box was completely demolished when closed circuit television was introduced in October 1981. *John Scrace.*

"On leaving the viaduct the next object worthy of note is Bitterne Station – a neat red brick building which is conveniently accessible to Bitterne and its neighbourhood. The public road has been raised about 14 feet and carried over the railway by means of an iron girder bridge. At this place peeps are obtained of some very beautiful scenery, the water stretching out to the right, and the picturesque wooded district to the left. The line eventually rises towards Itchen, crosses the road to the village and over Pear Tree

Green road in a similar manner, the latter has been lowered to the extent of about 16 feet for the purpose. The building at Woolston is a model to that provided at Portswood. A short distance beyond the line passes through a cutting 25 feet deep emerging at Miller's Pond, the road leading to Sholing being crossed by a three arched bridge and the turnpike road from Bursledon to the Floating Bridge by an ornamental arch girder. Another cutting is entered and after passing under another road leading to Woolston the line runs parallel with the road to Hound and terminates at the rear of the Gas Works connected with Netley Hospital".

The service to Netley in 1866 provided for eight trains each way on weekdays and three on Sundays.

In the above account mention was also made that a Bill was being prepared for the line to be continued from Netley over the River Hamble by a swing bridge through to Warsash, Titchfield and Fareham, but powers to extend the line to Fareham on the present route were not finally obtained until 1883, and the extension was opened on 2nd September 1889. Even then the line remained single with crossing loops at Bitterne, Netley and Swanwick, until 1901 when a crossing loop was provided at Woolston. Following alterations made at St. Denys in 1899, a new down line was brought into use between Adelaide Road Crossing and Bitterne on 27th February 1910, when the existing single line became the up line. On 10th April 1910 a new down line was brought into use between Bitterne and Woolston when the existing single line became the up line, while double line working was introduced between Woolston and

One of the Brighton Atlantics (4-4-2) No. 32431 *South Foreland* on a Bournemouth to Brighton train approaching the viaduct over the River Itchen between St. Denys and Bitterne. *Author's collection*

Netley on 29th May 1910. The line to Fareham being completely doubled by April 1911.

In 1957 the steam trains on local services were replaced by diesel electric multiple units, resulting in a much improved service both in timings and frequency.

Colour light signalling and track circuit block working was introduced over the line on 9th March 1980, eliminating the semaphore signalling and the remaining signal boxes. During 1989 preparations for electrification of the line from St. Denys to link up with the Portsmouth Direct electrified lines were carried out prior to electric train services being introduced during May 1990.

A double headed excursion train from Cheltenham to Portsmouth passing through Bitterne on 10th June 1956. The leading engine is No. 6384, a 2-6-0 of the 4300 class, No. 6320 is behind. *L. Elsey*

Bitterne station entrance with the small coal office for the Colliery Supply Company Ltd. *M. Snellgrove collection*

Bitterne

The station was opened in March 1866 as Bitterne Road, being given its present name in November 1896. A crossing loop was provided to enable trains to cross each other on the single line, and this is somewhat surprising as Woolston would have been nearer the midway point between Portswood and Netley, but it may have been provided at Bitterne to assist the working at Portswood, bearing in mind that originally the Branch trains there were dealt with on the main line.

The station building on the down platform was enlarged in 1902, and about the same time land was acquired to improve the small goods yard which was served by a connection in the crossover which was provided at the St. Denys end of the station. This resulted in making Bitterne yard a somewhat difficult place to carry out shunting operations for it was necessary to obstruct both the up and the down lines. Fortunately the yard only held a maximum of 18 wagons so the number of wagons involved at any one time was quite small. For a number of years there was a short private siding off the goods yard to serve the British Petroleum Company.

Alterations were made to the road overbridge at the Woolston end of the station in 1910 and again in 1931/2.

The railway company did not perform road deliveries

Bitterne station looking back towards St. Denys. A pre-First World War view.

M. Snellgrove collection

connection at the St. Denys end of the station. Included in this acquisition was the residence which eventually became No. 117 Macnaughten Road, and this was allocated as the station master's residence, while the previous accommodation used by him above the station building was let to other railway staff. Until 1903 passengers crossed the line from one platform to the other by a foot crossing, but the present footbridge was erected during that year.

When the line from Adelaide Road Crossing to Bitterne was doubled in February 1910 an additional siding was provided at the back of the down platform, and at the same time the connection to the yard was made from a slip

from Bitterne, these being carried out by an Agent, who for many years was a Mr. Rockett of Pound Street, Bitterne.

The goods yard was closed on 13th July 1959, and the track was removed in 1962, and since then various light industrial firms have developed on part of the site. Electric lighting took the place of gas lighting in 1968. The signal box on the down platform was taken out of use on 10th October 1966, and was demolished during 1969.

When the electric service was introduced in May 1990 the station became unstaffed. A small waiting shelter was provided on the down platform, while the wooden shelter on the up platform was replaced by a smaller shelter.

Above: Another view of Bitterne – this time looking towards Woolston showing the station building on the left and also the signal box. A small goods yard consisting of two sidings existed to the left of the photograph.   *Author's collection*

Below: Hampshire diesel multiple unit No. 204001 at Bitterne on a stopping Southampton–Portsmouth Harbour service on 13th June 1987.   *I.J. Bovey*

Woolston

The provision of a station at Woolston was included in the 1863 Act mainly as a result of objections to the proposed railway being made by the Itchen Floating Bridge Company. The existing station building on the up platform was erected when the line was opened, and is practically an exact copy of the building at St. Denys, except that the Woolston building is now covered with stucco.

Originally there was no crossing loop at Woolston, but it was obvious that by the end of the last century the demand for improved facilities was such that land had been acquired to enable the goods yard to be extended and in January 1901 a crossing loop was brought into use together with the signal box on the up platform.

The down siding at the Netley end of the station was extended on 4th January 1910 towards Netley, and on the

Above: Woolston station looking towards Sholing with the original open type footbridge. Note the milk churns on the 'up' platform.
Robert Humm & Co.

Left: Woolston station building of 1866 and the signal box of 1901.

Woolston Station – the building on the 'up' platform was built in 1866, while the signal box beyond was not erected until 1901.
Author's collection

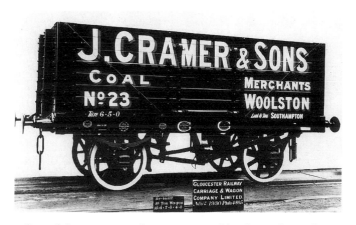

One of the ten ton coal wagons owned by the coal merchant J. Cramer & Sons of Radstock Road, Itchen, who operated from the goods yard at Woolston for many years. *H.M.R.S.*

their steel plates and other heavy equipment by rail, and during the Second World War the yard crane was replaced by an electrically operated crane. Several coal merchants had storage accommodation in the yard.

During an air raid in November 1940 the 5.35 p.m. Portsmouth & Southsea to Bristol, worked by engine No. 441, was hit by a bomb at Woolston station causing the death of one passenger – a Polish airman. The late Don Bradley in his books on LSWR Locomotives quotes the date of this incident as the 17th November, but this was a Sunday on which day the 5.35 p.m. Portsmouth & Southsea was not booked to run. Examination of the air raid records in Southampton Records Office and those held by Southampton City Technical Services have been made, and although no mention is made of the incident, it would seem that the most likely date when this incident occurred was Saturday 23rd November on which night the town suffered a very heavy raid, and the railway line at Woolston was damaged.

The Southern Region Civil Engineer arranged during the 1950s with Southampton Corporation for an area of land adjoining Pear Tree Green to be used as a tip for waste materials. A siding with a trailing connection was installed in the down line between Bitterne and Woolston on 29th August 1954, and this was operated from a Ground Frame. A number of sidings were provided in the Tip which was in use from December 1954 until August 1955, and again from June 1956 until June 1976. The sidings were subsequently removed and the connection and ground frame were removed on 12th December 1976.

The goods yard was closed to general traffic as from 7th March 1966, but remained in use for rail borne coal

23rd October of the same year it was extended further to a point about 470 yards from the signal box where a ground frame was provided to operate a new connection between the down siding and the down line. The double track between Woolston and Netley was brought into use on 29th May 1910.

The goods yard, consisting of four sidings, became a very busy place and a large goods shed with a 40 cwts. crane was erected together with a yard crane having a lifting capacity of 10 tons. For many years the shipbuilding firm of J.I. Thornycroft & Company received the majority of

The Bitterne end of Woolston station in 1903/4 showing the bridge over Bridge Road. This structure was rebuilt in 1904. The points in the right hand line lead to a siding while the second pair of points are at the end of the crossing loop and lead to the single line to Bitterne.

Author's collection

traffic until 2nd October 1966. After that date the coal merchants continued to use the yard, but the coal was brought in by road transport. The goods shed was let to the haulage company Solent Express.

The gas lighting on the station was replaced by electric lighting in 1968. Automatic colour light signalling was brought into use on 9th March 1980, when the signal box was closed. The lever frame has been removed, but the building still remains being rented by the Solent Model Railway Society.

During the latter part of 1985 the goods yard was cleared of all traders, the goods shed was demolished early in 1986. The land was subsequently sold and housing development took place, about forty houses being erected. If the tenants of some of these houses dig their gardens deep enough they are sure to find a good supply of coal dust!

In connection with electrification various alterations were made to the upside building in 1990 including the provision of a new ticket office at the Bitterne end of the building, and this enabled the major part of the 1866 building to be taken out of operational use.

Three car diesel electric unit 207010 working the 10.20 Southampton to Portsmouth Harbour on 20th March 1990 at Woolston showing the site of the former goods yard now occupied by houses.

I.J. Bovey

Sholing

In the report in the *Southampton Times* relating to the opening of the line to Netley on 5th March 1866 there is no mention of the existence of a station at Sholing. In May of the same year some of the local inhabitants suggested that a station should be provided near Millers Pond, and this was agreed. A temporary platform was erected on the downside of the single line as an experiment and was first used on 1st August 1866, and a small station building was subsequently provided on the platform. Access to the platform was gained from a footpath adjacent to the road overbridge at the Woolston end, which was constructed for a double line of railway.

No sidings or goods yard were provided, but it would seem that for a short period a small signal box did exist on the platform to operate signals, although it is not clear for how long this remained in existence. For a number of years Sholing had its own station master, and a house was erected at the junction of Station Road and Cranbury Road. In later years Sholing came under the control of the station master at Woolston, and the house, which still stands today, was sold out of railway ownership.

In 1910 a new platform and waiting shelter was provided on the upside of the line to serve the single line which became the up line when the line through the station was doubled in May 1910. Prior to this the platform and building on the downside was demolished to make room for the new down line, resulting in the construction of a new down platform and station buildings. Initially only short platforms were provided, but in October 1910 the platforms were extended to their present length – down platform to 528 feet and the up to 550 feet.

Although there was no goods yard, goods traffic was dealt with at the station until July 1932. It was limited in weight to a maximum of 3 cwts. and restricted to Road Box traffic only. The Road Boxes which normally contained traffic for several stations were attached to a goods train, which was booked to stop at Sholing and the traffic would be unloaded or loaded direct to and from the station platform.

Since 6th December 1965 the station has been unstaffed, but for a while passengers requiring tickets were able to purchase them from the Newsagent whose shop was adjacent to the station entrance. In July 1967 Southampton Model Railway Society rented the station building for use as a clubroom, and remained there until the end of 1985. Since then the building was left vacant and was regularly vandalised until February 1990 when it was completely demolished and replaced by a waiting shelter. A similar shelter was provided on the up platform.

Sholing Station prior to the doubling of the line in 1910. It will be noted that the road bridge had been constructed for two lines, and to enable the second line to be laid in a new platform was built on the ground in the foreground. The 'down' platform and building was then demolished and a new platform and building erected. In those days it was quite frequent to find old coach bodies on platforms and in yards being used for stores etc. The house on the right hand end of the road bridge was the station master's residence and the house remains today although not now in railway ownership.   *Author's collection*

Southampton Town Quay & Royal Pier

The opening of the LSWR line from London to Southampton in May 1840 brought the railway to within one mile of the Royal Pier and even less to the Town Quay which were both under the control of Southampton Harbour Commissioners.

On 26th May 1845 the Commissioners considered a proposal for the provision of a tramway from the Town Quay to the railway terminus. An approach was made to Southampton Dock Company and to Southampton Corporation as to whether land could be made available for a tramway. Contact was also made with the Railway Company as to the most convenient point where the tramway could join the railway.

The Dock Company were not prepared to help, stating

in their reply that such a tramway would be more or less a thoroughfare through the most valuable and important portion of the Company's land for the conveyance of traffic entirely unconnected with the Docks and would be destructive of the protection and security for which they in common with all Docks were expressly closed.

The Corporation did, however, agree to the tramway being laid on their land immediately in front of the Dock Company's property. As it was the intention to work the tramway with horses it was decided to connect the tramway with the main railway by means of a wagon turntable located in Canute Road.

Mr. G.L. Emett was given the contract to construct the tramway together with two turntables, one in Canute

South Western Hotel under renovation about the turn of the century. One of the rail crossings into the Old (Eastern) Docks can be seen in the foreground. The building on the right is Canute Road crossing box.   *Author's collection*

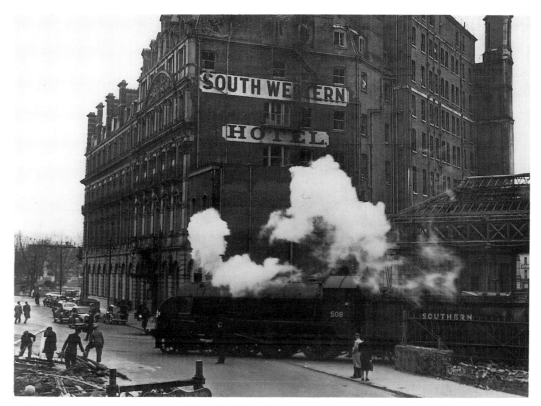

Above: A freight train hauled by Urie 'S15' No. 508 crosses Canute Road on 23rd November 1940 with the damaged South Western Hotel and Terminus station behind.

Associated British Ports courtesy Southampton City Museums

Below: As a result of the main line between Southampton Tunnel Junction and Southampton Tunnel being blocked by air raid damage on 8th July 1941, for at least one day the Waterloo to Bournemouth trains were diverted via Canute Road, the Docks and Harbour Board lines to Southampton Central via the Millbrook exit. The photograph below shows one such train hauled by No. 774 *Sir Gaheris* passing through No. 3 Dock Gate into the Old (Eastern) Docks.

Author's collection

Left: Adams 'B4' 0-4-0T No. 30096 crossing Canute Road from the Old (Eastern) Docks with an LCGB railtour on 6th April 1963. The handsignalman with his bell and flag is protecting the train.
Roger Hardingham collection

Below: 'Down' boat train worked by West Country class No. 34009 *Lyme Regis* passing Canute Road crossing box on 31st May 1956.
Associated British Ports courtesy Southampton City Museums

'U' class No. 31802 works a freight train out of the Old (Eastern) Docks via No. 3 Dock Gate across Canute Road on 12th July 1956. The open space behind the locomotive is where Dock House was constructed in 1962.   *D.H. Cull*

Southampton Canute Road crossing box in July 1970. This building was brought into use in December 1955. The previous box was immediately opposite on the other side of the lines. The box was taken out of use in 1981 when flashing road lights were installed.   *John Scrace*

Road and the other at the Town Quay, and the estimated cost was £1,800. The work was completed by 31st December 1847 and the actual cost was £1,902 – 9s – 5d.

In 1851 the tramway was leased to the LSWR for £20 per annum, but the Harbour Commissioners were still responsible for the maintenance. Two years later the Town Quay was extended and the sidings lengthened accordingly.

In 1858 the lease was renewed on a new basis for four years, rent free, the Railway Company to keep the tramway in repair and pay a bonus of £30 to the Commissioners.

Stothert & Pitt Ltd. of Bath installed an improved turntable at the Town Quay in 1862, the cost of which was met by the Commissioners.

During September 1870 it was reported that South-

Southampton Royal Pier in the 1880s showing the single track and a train at the platform. The Pier was completely reconstructed in 1891/2 when canopies were provided on both platforms.
Courtesy John Attwood

Left: The railway on the Royal Pier at Southampton at about the turn of the century. The platforms are now equipped with canopies. Normally the right hand platform was used as this was more convenient for the passengers, while the other line was used mainly by the engine to run round its train. *Pamlin Prints*

Below: The Royal Pier in about 1919/20 showing the portion of the railway track which needed repair. It would seem that possibly during the First World War it had been damaged by a ship. The train service to the Pier was never restored and the track was subsequently removed. *Author's collection*

THE PIER, SOUTHAMPTON. 348.

Southampton Royal Pier – a train can be seen at the station. During the early 1900s when excavations were being carried out for the construction of No. 6 drydock and also for the White Star Dock (later renamed Ocean Dock) much of the waste material was used to reclaim land on which Pirelli General Cable Works were eventually built. In order to move the material to the site a temporary railway extension was made from the Harbour Board lines along the Esplanade, and this photograph shows the temporary line. Part of this area of water was later reclaimed and is now Mayflower Park. *Author's collection*

Right: One of the three special locomotives acquired to operate the
Town Quay and Royal Pier services.
Southampton standing in the sidings
at the Terminus station about
1901/2 – the locomotive was withdrawn from the Royal Pier service
in 1907, but was then used at various depots being finally sold in 1915
to Kynoch Ltd for use at Long-
parish, being finally scrapped in
about 1920. In the background is
South Western Chambers on the
corner of St. Lawrence Road leading to the Goods Depot. To the
right are Maritime Chambers showing the LSWR crest at the top of the
building which was completed in
1899. *C.H. Eden courtesy E.W. Fry*

Below: Former LB & SC Railway's
E2 – No. 32101 with a shunt movement on the Harbour Board lines
proceeding to the Old (Eastern)
Docks in May 1957. *H.C. Casserley*

ampton Council were in favour of granting the LSWR
permission to make a tramway across Canute Road to link
up with the Town Quay tramway, and so do away with the
turntable, and this would then enable the railway company
to run carriages from the terminus to the Royal Pier. The
local builders Bull & Sons carried out the work, together
with the extension of the line from the Town Quay to the
Royal Pier, the cost being about £3,000.

The *Southampton Observer* for the 4th February 1871
announced with regret the withdrawal of the horse omnibus
that had for so many years plied between the railway terminus, the West End station and the Royal Pier to various
hotels in the town, and this caused much inconvenience to
numerous commercial gentlemen. The omnibuses had

been operated by the Matcham family of the Royal and
Dolphin hotels ever since the railway had opened. As a
result of the withdrawal the LSWR were forced to run one
omnibus, which was brought down from London, to operate the service between the terminus and the Royal Pier for
the purpose of conveying their through booked passengers.

The *Southampton Times* reported that the new line to
the Royal Pier was formally opened on 25th September
1871, when the Traffic Manager of the LSWR, Mr. A.
Scott, arrived at Southampton by the 5.36 a.m. train from
London, and with several other people including Mr. Snow-
don, the Inpector of Ways, and Mr. J.W. Dyson, the Station
Superintendent, were conveyed from the ticket platform to
a spot not far from the Pierhead in railway carriages drawn

In April 1922 LSWR 0-4-0T No. 741 shunts on the Harbour Board lines at the Town Quay. This locomotive together with No. 744 served the Town Quay until 1957. In Southern Railway days the locomotive eventually became No. 3741 and in BR days became No. 30588.

H.C. Casserley

Left: No. 30588 shunting on Town Quay on 22nd March 1951.

S.W. Baker

Below: The engine crew of No. 30588 – 26th April 1957.

R.C. Riley

After the First World War the portion of line to the Town Quay which passed in front of the dock's property was used as sidings and here we have No. 30570 shunting on these sidings on 12th May 1951. *J.R. Purkess*

by three horses. The tramway was opened for traffic on the following day, two carriages, a first class and a second class, together with a wagon for luggage, were provided and the motive power consisted of three horses.

In the early 1870s extreme difficulty was experienced in operating the Tramway with horses owing to the large number of wagons which were then passing to and from the Town Quay and the station. In one month, November

1872, 313 loaded wagons were taken to the Quay and 293 loaded wagons left the Quay. By November 1875 the numbers had increased to 500 and 580 respectively. Some of this traffic involved the Clyde Shipping Company whose coastwise services then terminated at Southampton, and traffic to and from London passed via the LSWR. The Shipping Company extended their services to London in 1884. Early in 1876 an application was made by the Railway

When the two 'C14' Nos. 30588 and 30589 were withdrawn from service they were replaced for a few months by 77s, the Redbridge Works shunter, and here the locomotive is shunting the same sidings, this time on 14th December 1957. *I.J. Bovey*

Company to the Council for permission to operate a steam engine between the station and the Town Quay and Royal Pier to meet the requirements of the increasing trade.

The Council gave permission for steam working initially for one year, subject to the following conditions:–

a) That the speed of the engine be limited to 5 m.p.h.

b) That the Railway Company provide a man with a red flag and bell to warn the public when the engine crosses the public way.

c) That the engine be specially constructed for the purpose on the same principle as the locomotives in the Docks, with powerful brakes and that the exhaust steam should be discharged into the tank.

d) That the weight of the engine in full trim should not exceed the maximum weight of the trucks when loaded, viz 13 tons.

The LSWR ordered a suitable locomotive from Shanks & Sons of Arbroath at the cost of £995, an 0–4–0 tank engine with three foot wheels and a wheel base of 5'6". It entered service on 21st September 1876 and was named *Southampton*. In the *Southampton Times* for 30th September 1876 it was reported that the locomotive had proved a great advantage to the working between the station and the Town Quay/Royal Pier and went on to say that it could pull 25 loaded wagons. Horses still remained working on the Town Quay itself owing to the poor state of the permanent way there.

A second similar locomotive was supplied by Shanks in 1877, and this was given the name of *Cowes*. By 1879 it was considered that a third engine was required and at the time a suitable locomotive was available for sale in Southampton Docks having been returned from Germany where it had been used for constructional work. This engine was acquired for £450 and was already named *Ritzbuttel*, and somewhat surprisingly retained that name.

Under section 4 of the Locomotive Act of 1865 it was unlawful to drive any locomotive along a public highway at a speed greater than 4 mp.h., or through a town or village at more than 2 m.p.h. In April 1881 a Mr. J.J. Myers brought a case against the LSWR concerning the speed of the engine *Southampton* working along Canute Road. The case was proved and a fine of 1s/– was imposed. The LSWR appealed to a higher court, but the decision still went against them, so it was recommended that the whole matter should be reviewed. Up to this time the Board of Trade had been somewhat reluctant to give their consent to the steam working, but in the Southampton Harbour Act of 1882 the working was adequately covered with a number of requirements being stipulated as follows:–

1) The engines used on the Tramway shall comply with the following requirements:

a) They shall be fitted with an efficient brake.

b) The Name or Number of each engine shall be shown in a conspicuous part thereof.

c) Each engine shall be fitted with suitable life-guards to push aside obstructions and with a whistle or bell to be sounded as a warning as necessary.

d) Arrangements shall be made enabling the Driver or (when the engine is running chimney first) Assistant to be in immediate communication with the Driver to command the fullest possible view on the road before him.

e) Each engine shall so far as practicable be free from noise produced by blast and all fire used on the engine shall be concealed from view.

2) The speed at which the engine and carriages shall be driven or propelled along the tramways shall not exceed the rate of five miles an hour.

3) The whistle or bell shall be sounded by the driver of the engine from time to time when it is necessary as a warning.

4) No smoke or steam shall be emitted from the engine so as to cause a nuisance to either passengers or to the public.

5) Whenever it is necessary to prevent impending danger the engine shall be brought to a standstill.

6) The speed at which the engines and carriages shall cross or pass along Canute Road shall not exceed three miles an hour.

7) During traffic hours of the Southampton Street Tramways the engines and trains on the passenger and goods lines shall be brought to a standstill before crossing Canute Road.

In 1884 the LSWR made an application to improve the curves on the tramway so that it would take six–wheeled carriages.

Between 1890 and 1892 the Royal Pier was considerably enlarged and improved and during this work a covered platform was constructed. At the same time the Town Quay was extended by about 850 feet to its final length. The new Pier was opened on 2nd June 1892 although the whole of the work was not completed until the following year. About 1896 an additional track was laid from the terminus to the Town Quay.

During the early part of this century a temporary extension was made from the Harbour Board lines along the roadway towards the site later occupied by Pirelli General Cable Works to enable material excavated during the construction of No. 6 drydock and the White Star Dock (later known as Ocean Dock) to be conveyed to that site for land reclamation.

In 1898 the locomotive *Southampton* was transferred to work on Poole Quay, and *Cowes* and *Ritzbuttel* were subsequently replaced by two locomotives originally belonging to the Southampton Dock Company – they were *Clausentum* and *Ironside* which were in 1901 transferred for use on the Town Quay and Royal Pier services. From about 1912 one of Drummond's steam rail motors was regularly used on the passenger service, while Class C14's Nos. 743/4/5 were used on the Town Quay. About 1912 all movements of freight traffic to and from the Town Quay passed via the Dock lines instead of the public roadway, the Dock route being retained until the end of working in May 1970.

The passenger train service between the terminus station and the Royal Pier was somewhat limited. In 1897 there were five trains each way on weekdays. Four years later there were seven trains to the Pier, but only six from the Pier on weekdays, and three on Sundays. By 1914 there were five to the Pier and six back, with only two on Sundays.

Just prior to the outbreak of war in August 1914 the portion of the pier on which the railway was situated was in need of extensive repairs. According to most reports the passenger train service to and from the Royal Pier was withdrawn by the end of September 1914, although there is some doubt as to the actual date, for Bradley in his book on LSWR locomotives states that a steam rail motor was allocated to the service in 1915. The lines on the Pier were, however, used by the military during that war. Like the Docks the Town Quay was also fully involved during the First World War with military traffic and by 1917 there was

USA Dock tank No. 30067 with a shunt movement along the Harbour Road lines from the New (Western) Docks to the Old (Eastern) Docks on 2nd June 1962.   *E.W. Fry*

a considerable movement of barges to and from the Continent with such traffic.

After the First World War the passenger train service was never restored and as all freight movements were passing via the Dock lines, the portion of the tramway between the terminus station and the main dock entrance became disused, while the portion from the main dock gate towards the Town Quay was used as sidings. The former portion remained and was again used during the Second World War, but was finally removed in April 1952.

After the First World War Class C14s locomotives Nos. 0741 and 0744 worked the Town Quay regularly, being renumbered 3741 and 3744, and on nationalisation 30588 and 30589, being finally withdrawn in 1957. Redbridge Works shunter No. 77S (formerly 745) then performed the shunting until it was replaced by a diesel shunting engine in 1959.

In connection with the construction of the New Docks (Western Docks) one of the Harbour Board lines was extended at the end of the 1920s to the New Docks site across the front of the entrance to the Royal Pier. A large number of trains passed via this route until the access at Millbrook was completed in June 1935. These workings caused many complaints from the regular users of the Town Quay for

when the shunters were involved with the movements of the Dock trains, the shunting of wagons on the Town Quay was often delayed. Traffic to and from the Town Quay was then still quite heavy averaging a daily figure of 80 loaded wagons to and about 90 loaded from the Quay.

After June 1935 when the Millbrook access to the New Docks was brought into use the Harbour Board lines were still regularly used for shunting movements between the Old and the New Docks, but only very rarely for loaded passenger trains. Owing to air raid damage at St. Marys in July 1941 the main line passenger services from Waterloo to Bournemouth were diverted via that route for at least one day.

With the decline in coastal trading on the Town Quay the freight service was eventually withdrawn on 4th May 1970, but transfer movements between the Eastern and Western Docks continued to pass, but this link was finally closed in October 1979, and a road traffic island was constructed across the track at the Town Quay and traffic lights installed.

The Town Quay/Royal Pier area is now in the process of being developed for offices, shops and a marina, which will totally change the whole character of this area.

Above: 'H15' class No. 474 with the head code of 'Special boat train Waterloo to Southampton Docks' hauls a train including some Pullman cars along the Harbour Board lines from the New (Western) Docks to the Old (Eastern) Docks. The actual date of the photograph is not known, but if it was before June 1935 the train could well have been a loaded one. After that date the Millbrook access was available and normally loaded passenger trains passed via that route. *Author's collection*

Below: Southampton Town Quay and Harbour Board lines in the late 1930s. Plenty of railway wagons emphasising the large amount of rail borne traffic which was then still passing through the Town Quay. The line at the bottom right hand corner is the extension leading to the New (Western) Docks. *Courtesy John Bell*

Railways of Southampton Docks

A view of Southampton Docks in the late 1880s taken from the top of South Western Hotel. The then two existing rail connections across Canute Road can be clearly seen with the railway serving the Outer Dock (centre background) and the Inner Dock on the right. The large building on Canute Road was the Dock Office and the smaller building in front was the residence of the Dock's Engineer. On the latter site Maritime Chambers was constructed in 1899.

Associated British Ports courtesy of Southampton City Museums

If the people involved with the planning of the London & Southampton Railway had had their way the Docks would have been developed as part of the railway system, but as they were unable to raise sufficient funds for the construction of the docks as well as the railways the proposals for the docks were omitted.

In May 1836 an Act authorising the newly formed Southampton Dock Company to construct a dock at Southampton was passed by Parliament, and the foundation stone was laid on 12th October 1838. The London & Southampton Railway Act of 1837 included the provision of a railway connection to the proposed dock. The quays which eventually formed part of the Outer Dock, were first used in August 1842, and by then a railway line had already been laid across Canute Road for it was stated on that inaugural occasion that it was possible to discharge cargo from the ship into railway wagons for conveyance direct to London.

Initially the Southampton Dock Company did not own any locomotives and it would seem doubtful at that time whether the Railway Company's locomotives did actually cross Canute Road. The Dock Company had a contract with a Mr. Matchem to supply six horses for performing shunting in the Docks. There is evidence available as late as 1863 that horses were used to haul passenger carriages into the Docks for in March of that year the Prince of Wales married Princess Alexandra of Denmark and they travelled to Southampton en route to Osborne House in the Isle of Wight for their honeymoon, and when the special train arrived at Southampton, the engine was detached at the Ticket platform on the north side of Bridge Road level crossing and several horses were attached to the carriages and vans to take them into the Docks for the Royal couple to join the Royal yacht *Fairy*.

It would seem that the Dock Company did not own any wagons for at the Officers' Committee meeting of the LSWR held on 15th August 1865, Mr. Scott suggested that as Southampton Dock Company were in the habit of using the Company's wagons in the Docks, about twelve old wagons should be offered to them at £35 each.

In the 1850s the Docks were enlarged with the opening of a non-tidal basin, later to be known as the Inner Dock

Clausentum, the Roman name for Southampton, one of the locomotives built for the Southampton Dock Company in 1890 by Hawthorn Leslie & Co., shown here as LSWR No. 457. Transferred to the duplicate list in 1908 it was then 0457. In 1914 it was renumbered 734 and was finally withdrawn in September 1945, having in addition to working in Southampton Docks also worked on the Royal Pier, and then later on Poole Quay Tramway, and shed pilot at Bournemouth and Guildford and during the Second World War assisted in the Admiralty sidings at Bedenham, Gosport, from time to time.

Author's collection

and a second line of railway was provided across Canute Road. The traffic passing through the Docks continued to increase so much that it was found that the horses were unable to adequately carry out the shunting work so in 1865 the Dock Company acquired its first locomotive, a small second hand engine with a vertical boiler from R. Brotherhood & Company of Chippenham for £350. It had been built in 1861 by Alexander Chaplin of Glasgow and was named *Chaplin*. This engine proved successful and enabled five horses to be dispensed with. During 1866 the permanent way in the Docks was gradually improved using partly used rails and sleepers provided on favourable terms by the LSWR. A second locomotive was in use by September 1866, an 0–4–0 well tank supplied by Simpson & Company, the London Agents of Henry Hughes. This locomotive was named *Osborne*. By the middle of 1870 a third locomotive was in use, a new 0–4–0–ST named *Canute* supplied by Dick & Stevenson of Airdrie. This engine arrived by sea in June 1870. *Chaplin* was replaced by another 0–4–0ST, this one named *Sir Bevis* was supplied by Shanks & Sons of Arbroath at the cost of £840 and was in service in 1872. Later the same year a repeat order was given to Shanks & Sons and this engine was named *Ascupart*. In the report of the half yearly meeting of Southampton Dock Company held on 9th August 1871 the Chairman stated that "a stable had been built for the new engines for although steam engines do not wish to be fed like horses they require equal protection and must be looked after if we are to preserve them".

The amount of shipping using the Docks continued to grow, and with it the amount of cargo being handled – in 1871 a total of 2,362 ships used the Docks, and 26,882 wagons (over 500 per week) were used for cargo, in addition there were 3,483 wagons of coal, no doubt much of this was for bunkering ships – all coal burners in those days, and there were also 10,000 trucks with mail and specie. Two years later the number of wagons dealt with had practically doubled. From 1876 all shunting movements across Canute Road were hauled, but not so in 1872 for on 25th January of that year, a long train was being pro-

pelled into the Docks across Canute Road and it was reported in the local paper that owing to wet weather "the hollow of the metals were full of stones and gravel causing three wagons to be derailed. Before the engine could be stopped three massive pillars were knocked down and part of a wall damaged".

In 1878 two more 0–4–0ST locomotives were added to the fleet, being supplied new from Vulcan Foundry – they were named *Vulcan* and *Bretwalda*, the latter name being from the title given to the Saxon ruler of Britain.

By 1876 additional quays had been provided along the River Itchen, but the size of the ocean going steamers continued to increase and so the demand for more and larger docks continued. Another deep water dock was planned, but the finances of the Dock Company were such that they were unable to carry out the work. The LSWR became further involved with the Dock Company and provided a loan of £250,000 to enable the Empress Dock to be built. The dock which provided additional quay frontage of 3,800 feet was opened on 26th July 1890 by Her Majesty Queen Victoria. At about the same time an additional line was laid in across Canute Road to serve the Empress Dock and this line is today the sole remaining railway link across Canute Road serving the Old (Eastern) Docks.

In 1890 two more 0–4–0ST engines were supplied – this time by Hawthorn Leslie & Company – they were named *Clausentum* and *Ironside*.

Further extensions to the Docks were planned, but money was not available, and so on the 1st November 1892 the LSWR acquired the Docks for £1,360,000 and immediately went ahead with a large investment scheme for providing additional quays and warehouses. As a result of the acquisition of the Docks the locomotives *Vulcan*, *Bretwalda*, *Clausentum* and *Ironside* were transferred to the LSWR being allocated the numbers – 118, 408, 457 and 458 respectively. *Ironside* lasted into British Railway days being finally scrapped at Eastleigh in 1954. On 8th August 1893 three special trains were run from Waterloo to Southampton Docks to enable the shareholders to inspect the Docks.

Above: Possibly the major traffic dealt with by the railway through Southampton Docks for many years was the various imports from South Africa, usually loaded to Nine Elms. Here we have bundles of skins and hides, and bales of wool – all from South Africa being loaded into railway wagons in 1921/2.
Associated British Ports courtesy Southampton City Museums

Below: The principal shunting yard in the Old (Eastern) Docks was Empress Yard. Here in September 1937 an Adams B4 is carrying out shunting operations.
Associated British Ports courtesy Southampton City Museums

Above: In the early 1930s what is now Mayflower Park was used for storage for much of the construction material used in conjunction with the building of the New (Western) Docks. A contractor's locomotive, one of eighteen such locomotives involved, is working and there is also a narrow gauge railway in use. In the middle distance alongside the Royal Pier are the paddlers *Queen, Bournemouth Queen* and *Solent Queen* and beyond are the four funnelled *Mauretania* and the three funnelled *Majestic.*

Left: The construction of the King George V Graving dock at the Millbrook end of the New (Western) Docks was a massive work involving two million tons of earth being removed and about ¾ of a million tons of concrete being used. Many contractor's locomotives were operating and one of them can be seen here in the background, about 1932.

Both Associated British Ports courtesy Southampton City Museums

The Southern Railway's 150 ton floating crane at Southampton was used during the 1920s and 1930s to convey locomotives and rolling stock to the Isle of Wight via Medina Wharf. Here we have a number of coaches being loaded by the crane at Southampton in 1936/7. The crane was officially registered as 'S.R. Floating Crane No. 1'. In the background the paddle steamer *Solent Queen* makes her way to the Royal Pier.

Associated British Ports courtesy Southampton City Museums

Another consignment of locomotives and rolling stock were taken by the floating crane to Medina Wharf on 13th April 1949 including two Adams '02' class W35 *Freshwater* (formerly No. 181) and W36 *Carisbrooke* (formerly No. 198) together with eight coaches.

Author's collection

Adams '02' class W14 *Fishbourne* (formerly No. 178) being unloaded by the floating crane at Medina Wharf in the Isle of Wight in May 1936.

Associated British Ports courtesy Southampton City Museums

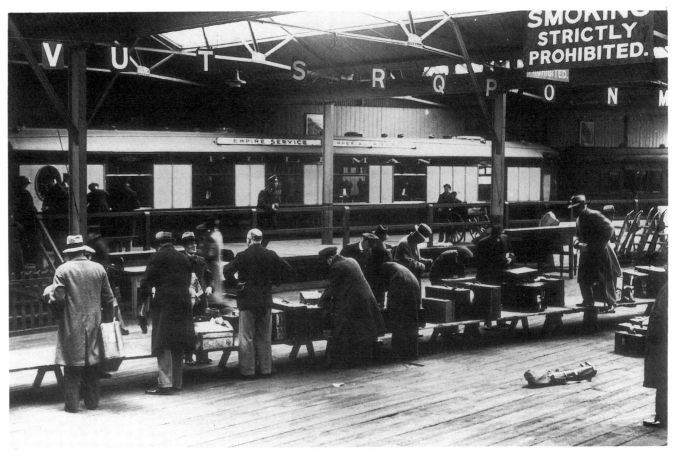

Above: Customs examination in progress in the shed at 50 berth for passengers who had arrived by Imperial Airways flying boat in 1937. The passengers had been brought from the flying boat to the berth by launch. The Pullman car in the background is labelled 'Empire Services – Imperial Airways'.

Southampton City Museums

Left: The New Docks (later the Western Docks) was provided with an engine turntable at the back of 108 shed, something which never existed in the Old Docks. This photograph shows 'Lord Nelson' class No. 855 *Robert Blake* being used to carry out the initial tests on the turntable in 1936. The turntable which was built by Ransomes & Rapier Ltd, was 70' in length, and when no longer required in the docks was acquired in 1976 by the Great Western Society and can now be seen at the Didcot Steam Centre.   *Author's collection*

The same year the American Line transferred their North Atlantic service from Liverpool to the port. Normally two boat trains were operated every Saturday from Waterloo for the sailing of that Company's ships – the first train was booked two minutes at Northam station to enable tickets to be collected, while tickets on the second train were collected at Waterloo before departure.

Other regular boat trains operating at the time were for Royal Mail Steam Packet Company, the Union Line and the German Norddeutscher Lloyd, while five freight trains were booked to work out of the Docks each weekday – two of these for Willesden.

Traffic continued to increase more powerful locomotives were required so the end of 1893 saw the arrival in Southampton of four Adams B4 class 0–4–0Ts, the mainstay of the Docks shunting work for the next fifty years –

the locomotives were Nos. 81, 176, 96, 97 and were given the names *Jersey, Guernsey, Normandy* and *Brittany* respectively, all places having railway steamer links with the port. Within the next eight years eight more B4s were transferred to the Docks as follows :– 85 *Alderney*, 86 *Havre*, 89 *Trouville*, 90 *Caen*, 93 *St. Malo*, 95 *Honfleur*, 98 *Cherbourg* and 102 *Granville*, while two more were added in 1908 – *Dinard* and *Dinan*, both of the Drummond version.

At one time No. 3 shed was used as a depot for the locomotives, but later a locomotive shed was erected west of Nos. 1/2/3 drydocks. This shed was rebuilt in 1954 and remained in use until the 1970s.

In 1894 the LSWR made available facilities for dealing with troopships, and eventually the port became the principal port for peacetime trooping. Between the wars the trooping season lasted from September to April each year,

Above: A wartime photograph published in August 1944, but the background was deleted by the censor. W.D. No. 179 (ex GWR 2466) is shown and it is known that this locomotive was working in the Southampton Area in August 1944, and it is believed that the photograph was taken near the Royal Pier, where rail loading facilities were provided during the War.

Associated British Ports courtesy Southampton City Museums

Right: On 22nd September 1945 a special ceremony was held at 104 berth in the New (Western) Docks for the naming of Merchant Navy class locomotive No. 21C19 *French Line – C.G.T.*. Many distinguished personalities were present and alongside the quay was the liner *Ile de France* which was being handed back to the French Line after wartime service with the allies. Part of the vessel can be seen.

Associated British Ports

A boat train including a Pullman car leaving 44 berth hauled by King Arthur class No. 739 *King Leodegrance* in April 1946. At the berth is the *Queen Mary* still in her wartime grey.

Associated British Ports

In August 1947, sixteen USA 0-6-0T engines were shipped on to the former tank landing ship *Empire Baltic* at Southampton for Split for the Yugoslav government arranged by UNRRA. Here two of the locomotives are shown in the hold.

Associated British Ports courtesy of Southampton City Museums

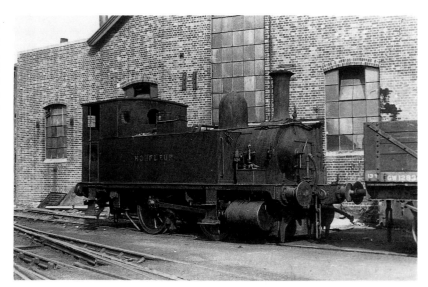

Right and below: Adams 'B4' class *Honfleur* working in Southampton on 21st September 1947 and on the same day (below) *Guernsey*, one of the first 'B4s' to work in the Docks, and USA 0-6-0T No. 72 are seen standing outside the small motive power shed in the Old (Eastern) Docks.   *Both by H.C. Casserley*

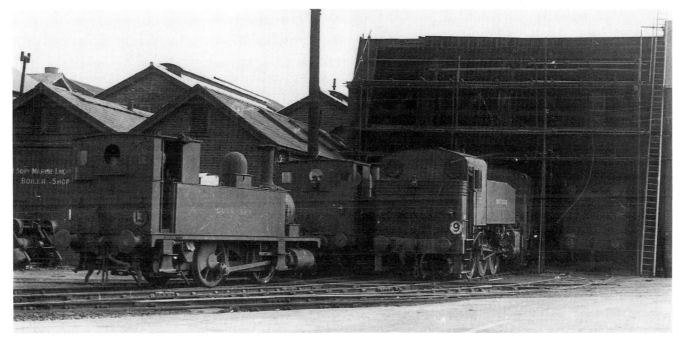

and many troop trains were run to cope with these movements. After the Second World War the troopships operated throughout the year until the end of 1962 by which time it was decided to use aircraft for all future peacetime movements.

In the majority of cases the running of boat trains were pre–arranged, but in 1898 this was not always the case for a report in the *Southampton Observer* for 11th June referred to the Wilson Furness Leyland Company's *Winifreda* – "A special train was arranged after the vessel left New York, and the passengers had no idea until they got to the Needles that they had the opportunity of saving a day by disembarking at Southampton, and travelling to London by train. The local manager met the ship off the Isle of Wight and explained the arrangements to the passengers and half of them accepted. The ship arrived in the Docks at 6.30 a.m. the train left at 7.30 a.m. and was in Waterloo station just after 9.00 a.m.".

Special events such as Naval Reviews at Spithead always involved the running of many extra trains to and from the Docks. For the Review held on 26th June 1897 to mark the Diamond Jubilee of Queen Victoria twenty nine addi-

tional trains were run from Waterloo to the Docks between 5.00 a.m. and 10.00 a.m. carrying approximately 18,500 passengers. In addition a number of the normal service trains to Southampton were run in duplicate. In order to deal with the special trains on that occasion a platform about 2,700 feet in length was constructed in the Docks. Most of the trains were formed of LSWR stock, but the directors of the Great Western Railway arrived in a train formed of GWR stock which included several sleeping cars. On the day of the event the level crossings at Canute Road, Chapel, Bevois Street, Mount Pleasant and Dukes Road were closed to road traffic between 7.00 a.m. and 11.30 a.m.

In June 1902 another review was scheduled to take place to mark the Coronation of King Edward VII and 58 special trains were booked to run on the day, but owing to the King being indisposed the review was postponed until August when the number of trains then operated was less than the original schedule.

At the turn of the century during the South African war of 1899 – 1902 the importance of Southampton as a trooping port was fully demonstrated, with its close con-

Above: A boat train with Pullman cars entering the Old (Eastern) Docks and heading for dockhead for the sailing of Union Castle's *Edinburgh Castle* on 3rd February 1949. The *Queen Mary* is at 46/7 berths – her temporary berth while the Ocean Terminal was under construction.

Associated British Ports

Left: Lord Nelson class No. 857 *Lord Howe* enters the New (Western) Docks at the Millbrook entrance with a boat train for Cunard White Star's *Aquitania* on 4th October 1949. At the time the *Aquitania* was carrying immigrants to Canada, but the liner was near the end of her days for she was sold for breaking up early in 1950. In the background the goods shed in Millbrook yard can be clearly seen and beyond that is the large Toogoods Seeds warehouse – a firm which provided Millbrook station with a considerable amount of railway traffic.

Associated British Ports

Right: War Department's 2-8-0 No. 042 being loaded at Southampton on to the heavy lift ship *Belpareil* for Egypt on 5th April 1952.

Associated British Ports courtesy Southampton City Museums

Below: USA 0-6-0T No. 30062 on a RCTS special train at 50 berth on 17th May 1953. *R.C. Riley*

Above: USA 0-6-0T No. 30069 shunting carriages in Southampton Western Docks on the lines leading to the Carriage Cleaning Shed on 2nd February 1963. J. Rank's Solent Mill is in the background. *M.J. Fox*

Below: No. 30071 shunting in Southampton Eastern Docks on 20th September 1965. Empress Marshalling yard is on the left and the Empress Dock on the right. *M.J. Fox*

Above: On 2nd May 1958, No. 30770 *Sir Prianius* (the last King Arthur class locomotive to be withdrawn from service) with a banana van train waiting to leave the Old (Eastern) Docks, is passed by a van train worked by 'U' class No. 31798. The building on the right still stands today, but it was for many years the Shipping Traffic Office through which was dealt all the commercial aspects, including invoicing at one time, for all the rail traffic passing through the docks.

Right: A Cunard boat train leaves the Ocean Terminal with the *Queen Mary* at her berth on 8th July 1958. The locomotive is No. 30850 *Lord Nelson* now preserved. As was quite usual with the boat trains one or two vans were next to the engine for passengers luggage.

Both Associated British Ports
courtesy
Southampton City Museums

Above: The 'Cunarder' leaves the Ocean Terminal with passengers off the *Queen Elizabeth* on 12th May 1964, the engine is No. 34088 *213 Squadron.*

Author's collection

Below: Schools class No. 30932 *Blundells* on a boat train for London passing the Shipping Traffic Office on the way to No. 3 Dock Gate in Canute Road on 20th September 1955.

Associated British Ports courtesy Southampton City Museums

Four of the principal types of locomotives which have served Southampton Docks over the years – Adams 'B4' 0-4-0T, USA 0-6-0T, ex LB & SCR 0-6-0T and a Ruston Hornsby diesel electric shunter. In the back is the liner *Canberra* in No. 7 King George V Graving Dock.   *The late G. Wheeler*

nection by rail to Aldershot many troop trains were operated. During that period 528,000 troops and 27,922 horses together with tons of stores passed through the port – all arriving by train.

The extension of the Docks continued with quays on the River Test and by 1905 there was a total of 31 miles of railway track on the Docks property. The next major step forward occurred two years later when the White Star Line decided to transfer their express North Atlantic service from Liverpool to Southampton. As a result the construction of the White Star Dock (renamed Ocean Dock in 1922) was completed in 1911.

During the First World War Southampton became No.1 Embarkation port for Europe. During that war over seven million troops, 850,000 horses, 3 1/2 million tons of stores together with 180,000 vehicles passed through the port, the majority of which were moved by the railway. Numerous ambulance trains were also run.

To expedite the working an extra line was laid across Canute Road in December 1914 making two parallel lines through No.3 Dock gate. Mount Pleasant Crossing, Chapel Crossing and Canute Road were closed throughout the war to road traffic, and after numerous complaints a footbridge was erected over the lines at Canute Road for pedestrians for the duration of the war.

In 1919 both Cunard Line and Canadian Pacific Steamships Ltd. transferred their express North Atlantic

services from Liverpool to Southampton, and this of course resulted in many more sailings on that route. During the summer season in the 1920s there were often over fifty passenger ships sailing each month to New York or Canada involving many additional boat trains.

During the late 1920s and 1930s the Southern Railway developed regular railway excursions to visit the docks and the large passenger liners. In 1928 there were over 70,000 visitors who arrived by train from all parts of the country or by railway owned paddle steamers from Portsmouth and the Isle of Wight.

The late 1920s saw the commencement of the construction of the New Docks (renamed Western Docks in 1965). A massive dock extension scheme involving an area of over 400 acres being reclaimed from the sea, to provide a self contained dock estate with 7,000 feet of deep water quays and miles of railway sidings to serve the sheds and marshalling yards. The constructional work involved the running of hundreds of material trains, in particular chalk from Micheldever. Three main contractors were involved – Sir Robert McAlpine & Sons for the quay and sheds, while the contract for the construction of King George V Graving Dock was shared between John Mowlem & Co. Ltd. and Edmund Nuttall Ltd., and at one time as many as eighteen contractors' locomotives were working on the site. The Southern Railway purchased for the use of the Docks Engineer's Department an 0–4–0 saddle tank locomotive to assist with their part of the new works. This engine was built in 1910 by Barclay (Works No.1188) and was named *The Master General*, after the Master General of Ordnance, having been built for Woolwich Arsenal. After the completion of the New Docks the locomotive was retained for use in the Engineer's Yard in the Docks, being replaced by a diesel engine in 1946.

Initially the New Docks area was linked with the Old Docks by an extension across the front entrance to the Royal Pier from the Harbour Board lines on the Town Quay, and what is now Mayflower Park was used as an assembly point for much of the constructional material.

The first ship to sail from the New Docks was the White Star Line's *Homeric* in December 1932, and from then until June 1935 all loaded passenger trains passed via the Harbour Board lines and No.3 Dock Gate in Canute Road. The connections at Millbrook were brought into use in June 1935 and after that date shunting movements between the two Docks continued via the Harbour Board lines, but it was a rarity for a loaded passenger train to pass by that route. In the New Docks a new six road carriage cleaning and warming shed was erected, and this could accommodate 72 coaches. In addition a 70' locomotive turntable, built by Ransomes & Rapier Ltd., was installed at the back of 108 berth. This turntable, which had little use, is now at the Great Western Society's Centre at Didcot, having been moved there in 1976.

The use of Pullman cars on certain boat trains was introduced in January 1931 and proved immediately popular with the passengers.

Fyffes bananas commenced to pass regularly through the port in 1931. In June 1933 60,804 stems of bananas were discharged on one day involving the use of 424 wagons. On the same day cargo from other ships brought the total of loaded wagons to 976 leaving the Docks in 19 hours – the following month 3,200 wagons were loaded with bananas averaging over 100 vans per day. In September 1934, 115,888 stems were loaded into 681 wagons in 21 working hours.

The August Bank Holiday periods were often particularly busy – on Friday 29th and Saturday 30th July 1932, there were a total of 24 passenger ships on the move, and in addition the Southern Railway steamers were taking many holiday makers to the Channel Islands and France, involving a total of 37 boat trains in 48 hours. This, all in addition to the normal extra holiday traffic passing on the railway. Many more extra trains were run for the Naval Reviews of 1935 and 1937, with the latter there were 48 trains from London to the Docks and 45 in the reverse direction. Cunard White Star's liner *Queen Mary* first arrived in Southampton on 27th March 1936 from her builders on the Clyde, and the Southern Railway were very quick to exploit this. Many excursions were run to the Docks to 'View the *Queen Mary*' – on the 29th March nineteen special excursions were run – even then excursionists were not allowed on board the liner, but walked round King George V Drydock in which the vessel was berthed.

From the end of 1936 until the outbreak of war Imperial Airways were operating flying boats from Southampton Water to various parts of the British Empire. Originally the aircraft passengers were conveyed from Waterloo in a first class Pullman car attached to the 7.30 p.m. Waterloo to Bournemouth West, the coach being

German Prisoners of War coming ashore from Landing Craft near the Royal Pier in March 1945. The temporary wartime rail link to enable rail vehicles to be shipped to France can be clearly seen leading to the Landing Craft on the left. *Associated British Ports courtesy of Southampton City Museums*

Above and below: The import of Fyffes bananas were dealt with in the Empress Dock and in 1960 the accommodation at 24/5 berths was modernised and these two photographs show the shed as it was in the 1960s. The bananas were unloaded by means of conveyor belts and in the upper picture some of the stems of bananas can be seen in one of the conveyor belts before being loaded into rail vans.

Both Associated British Ports

On 27th April 1964 – 'A4' class No. 60008 *Dwight D. Eisenhower* was shipped on to the United States Lines' cargo vessel *American Planter* at Southampton by the floating crane. The locomotive had been presented by the British Railways Board to the National Railroad Museum of Green Bay, Wisconsin, USA. No. 60008 was originally No. 4496 *Golden Shuttle* and was renamed by the LNER in 1945 to honour the name of the Allied Supreme Commander in Europe during the Second World War.

Author's collection

detached at Eastleigh and then worked specially forward to Southampton Terminus. The passengers were accommodated in the South Western Hotel for the night, but usually take–off time was 5.00 a.m. so it meant early rising for passengers. For a while in 1938 the take–off time was altered and this resulted in the passengers travelling in a special train from Waterloo, but this did not last very long and soon reverted to the previous arrangements. Commencing on 5th July 1939 a new Headquarters Terminal building was opened at Victoria station, and then a special train formed of a corridor composite brake coach, a Pullman car and a corridor guard's luggage van was booked to leave Victoria (platform 17) at 8.05 p.m., being due in Southampton Terminus at 9.48 p.m. The train was booked to run on Sundays, Tuesdays, Wednesdays, Thursdays and Fridays. In the opposite direction the train was booked to leave the New Docks exits at Millbrook at 1.23 p.m. The flying boat service ceased with the outbreak of war, but was re–commenced later from Poole.

January 1939 saw the shipment through Southampton of the LMSR *Coronation* No.6220 (actually No.6229 which had been renumbered and renamed) together with seven carriages of the Coronation Scot train for the New York World Fair.

The outbreak of war in September 1939 saw the elimination of the regular passenger shipping services, but Southampton became one of the principal embarkation and supply ports for the British Expeditionary Force, and during the early months of the war about 800,000 troops together with 300,000 tons of stores passed through the port. After Dunkirk and the collapse of France the Docks were closed to all ocean going shipping and as a result there was a comparatively quiet period so far as railway operations were concerned. By the end of 1942 Lease/Lend cargoes were beginning to arrive and the following year saw the massive build up for the 'D' Day operations. To assist with the increased traffic new connections were brought into use on 28th March 1943 to and from the New (Western) Docks at Redbridge, and these enabled trains to have a direct run to and from the Salisbury and Bournemouth lines.

During 1944/5 nearly four million troops and prisoners of war were passed through the port with three million tons of stores – the majority of which were moved by rail. Train ferries also returned to the port with two rail connections being made – one near the Royal Pier and the other adjacent to King George V drydock.

Immediately after the end of the war the Southern Railway acquired fourteen United States Transportation Corps 0–6–0T shunting engines to replace the ageing B4s. In addition several E1 and E2 classes 0–6–0Ts were transferred to the Docks, and for a while a couple of E4 0–6–2T were also working in the Docks.

The flying boat services returned to Southampton as from April 1946 by which time Imperial Airways had become part of British Overseas Airways Corporation. In 1948 a new Air Terminal was opened at 50 berth in the Old (Eastern) Docks and this was equipped to deal with rail traffic, but so far as is known it was never used for flying boat trains. BOAC withdrew their services in November 1950. Aquila Airways took over some of the operations until September 1958, but no special trains were run for that company.

Nationalisation initially brought very little change in the railway operations. Many of the shipping services returned to normal and during 1951 1,111 boat trains arrived in the Docks and 1,051 departed.

In 1952 the total track mileage in both Docks was equal to just over 77 miles. The wartime connections to the New (Western) Docks at Redbridge were taken out of use on 8th March 1953, although a portion of these lines remained for some years and the track bed was used to lay temporary lines to serve the tipping site in conjunction with the reclamation of land for the Container berths.

Throughout the 1950s and early 1960s rail traffic to and from the Docks was very heavy. With the sailings and arrivals of the *Queen Mary*, *Queen Elizabeth* and *United States* either three or four trains were involved including one complete Pullman car train, which was always the first to leave the Docks after the arrival of the ship and the last to leave Waterloo for a sailing. Several of the other boat trains regularly included one of more Pullman cars. The summer of 1952 saw the introduction of named boat trains such as *The Cunarder*, *The Statesman*, *Union–Castle Express*, *South American* and *Normandy Express*. The latter was later changed to *Brittany Express* and other names were introduced later, such as *Holland–American*.

On the 15th June 1953 another naval review took place in Spithead – this time for the Coronation of the present H.M. Queen – for which 28 special trains were run from Waterloo.

A somewhat unusual working from Southampton Docks applied during the 1950s. The boat train connection with the steamer service from Le Havre was booked to leave Southampton Docks at 7.03 a.m. on Sunday mornings and it was possible for ordinary passengers to join this train in the shed adjacent to the Continental Booking Office in the Outer Dock. For people living in the Southampton area, this train, which included a Pullman buffet car, was the first fast train to London on a Sunday morning. The train called at Eastleigh, Winchester and Basingstoke where ordinary passengers could also join the train. It was withdrawn in the early 1960s with the closure of the railway steamer services to Le Havre.

During 1955, 2,334 boat trains with 501,200 passengers were run together with 5,893 freight trains involving the use of 238,435 wagons. Among these figures was one day – 16th September when there were thirteen ships on the move needing 27 boat trains, six of these for railway owned ships. Two of the boat trains from the Docks were run to Victoria as Waterloo were unable to deal with them.

In 1963 a total of 1,727 boat trains were operated with 294,397 passengers and 4,997 freight trains were run with 180,561 wagons. By then road transport was beginning to take an equal share of the freight traffic, and by 1966 slightly more cargo was leaving the Docks by road than by rail.

In 1962 fourteen diesel electric shunting engines of 275 h.p. were ordered from Ruston & Hornsby to replace the steam engines which were gradually withdrawn.

Under the Transport Act of 1962 the British Transport Commission was abolished and British Transport Docks Board was established as an independent statutory authority thus divorcing the Docks entirely from railway ownership.

In June 1963, Pullman cars were withdrawn from all boat train workings. A post war record for freight train movements into and out of the Docks was established on 9th March 1964, when within a sixteen hour period, twenty five trains were run. Seventeen left the Docks with a total of 613 wagons conveying South African fruit, bananas and general cargo, while there were eight inward trains comprising of 293 loaded wagons.

The Maritime Freightliner terminal located to the rear of the container berths was opened in 1972 four long sidings were provided with connections from the down local line at Millbrook for inward trains and with the Up Dock Line at Millbrook for the outward trains. During 1987 approximately 60% of all the containers passing through the port of Southampton were handled by this terminal, so there is still a large quantity of shipping traffic passing by rail. Normally five or six trains operate in and out of the Terminal, six days a week.

Canute Road crossing box regulated movements into and out of Southampton Old (Eastern) Docks, and also to the Town Quay, in conjunction with the signalman at Southampton Yard box. This crossing box was originally sited on the downside of the lines leading to No.3 Dock Gate, but in December 1955 a new crossing box was erected on the upside immediately opposite the old box. Canute Road crossing has always been an open type crossing and the gates do not protect the movement of trains, and for many years the protection of trains crossing to and from the Docks was provided by a handsignalman with a flag or lamp and a bell, but in October 1981 flashing red lights were installed.

Track mileage in the Docks in 1967 was 66 miles, but ten years later it had been reduced to about half that figure. With the changing pattern of shipping operations, and in particular containerisation, the need for an extensive rail network is no longer necessary and so today there is only about five miles of track existing. In the Eastern Docks all that now remains is one line leading from Canute Road to serve the passenger terminal at 38/39 berths at Dockhead, the principal user of the Terminal being the *Queen Elizabeth 2* and normally only one boat train is required. In the Western Docks one line serves berths 105–108, and this is now normally used for occasional boat trains for cruise liners, in particular the P&O liner *Canberra*.

As to the future rail operations in the Docks, the Container trains to and from the Maritime Terminal should continue to operate for during 1991 the number of containers dealt with through the Container Terminal was 307,328, an increase of 22% over the number for 1990, and a fair proportion of these are still moved by rail. It would seem likely that the number of boat trains will continue to decline partly owing to higher operating costs and the increasing use of road transport.

Southampton Train Ferries

Early in January 1917 it was decided that it would be helpful to the war effort if a train ferry service was provided between this country and France to provide a quicker movement of military stores and equipment. Two terminals in England were selected, one at Richborough near Sandwich in Kent and the other in Southampton to ensure that it would be well clear of any German advance which might affect the French ports of Dunkirk, Calais and Boulogne. Three train ferries were ordered , two to operate from Richborough and the other one between Southampton and Dieppe, running three times each week. Each ferry had four lines of railway and was capable of taking a maximum of 54 wagons.

About 100 yards beyond the loops a marshalling yard was constructed on the gridiron system capable of holding about 500 wagons. There were twelve roads diverging from the two running lines. Eight berthing sidings also led out from this marshalling yard capable of holding a further 200 wagons, while a brick built engine shed with accommodation for two engines was provided at the north end.

At the southern end of the marshalling yard there was a connection to the Town Quay along the public road, this line was used very extensively to convey traffic to and from a service of barges which were operating from the Town Quay to France.

A signal box controlling movements on to and from

The train ferry jetty at Southampton about 1920. Soon afterwards the seaward end was dismantled and taken to Harwich for use of the train ferry service to the continent which was then being established from Harwich. *Courtesy of E.R.F. Hawkins*

The terminal facilities at Southampton were provided about 100 yards west (up river) from the Royal Pier, where a masonry pier approximately 100 yards in length was constructed to carry the rail tracks out to a timber viaduct and the link span. In view of the considerable movements of military traffic already passing through Southampton Docks it was decided to keep the Train Ferry traffic separate so the connection with the LSWR was made from the down bay line at Southampton West (later Central) station. The connection was operated from Ground Frame 'B' and the line was single for about 100 yards, when it became double track throughout to the jetty, about a mile away. At the station end of the line on ground at the back of the electricity power station there were seven sidings for the berthing and marshalling of wagons. The lines then passed behind Pirelli General Cable Works where there were two siding loops each capable of holding forty wagons, and a siding was constructed into Pirelli General Cable Works for their traffic.

the ferries was erected on an elevated bridge some 35 feet above the entrance to the ferry.

The service to Dieppe commenced operating on 13th December 1917.

About the middle of 1918 a new berth with three railway tracks was added to the existing facilities at Southampton so that an additional ferry could be accommodated. This vessel, known as TF4, operated between Southampton and Cherbourg, but did not enter service until 6th November 1918, a few days before the Armistice was signed. TF4 was different to the other three ferries as it had operated across the St. Lawrence River and was of the moveable deck type, and could only carry 33 wagons.

Military staff of the Inland Waterways & Dock Authorities Department were responsible for all operational movements between the LSWR Marshalling yard at the back of the electricity power station and the Train Ferry jetty, including the siding at Pirelli General Cable Works.

The train ferry jetty as completed in 1917 showing the two tracks leading to and from the jetty, both leading to and from the direction of the west station.

Author's collection

Both ferries continued to operate from Southampton until early in 1919 when the service was withdrawn. The total amount of railway equipment taken to France from Southampton was 8 locomotives, 42 coaches and 6,763 wagons, while 272 engines and 1,250 wagons were brought back from France. During the early 1920s the majority of the track was removed, but the remains of the jetty did not completely disappear until the 1930s with the construction of the New (Western) Docks.

The ferry TF4 was sold after the service was withdrawn, but the other three ferries were laid up and eventually acquired in 1923 by a new company Great Eastern Ferries Ltd. (later taken over by the London & North Eastern Railway Company) who operated them until 1939 between Harwich and Zeebrugge. The link span at Southampton was taken to Harwich in September 1923 for use in connection with this service.

During the Second World War train ferries returned to Southampton in connection with the invasion of Europe and used special facilities provided at 110 berth in the New (Western) Docks and also at the Town Quay/Mayflower Park. Among the vessels used were the three Southern Railway train ferries built in 1934/5 for the Dover–Dunkirk service.

It is of interest to note that the Southern Railway had plans to establish a permanent train ferry service from Southampton to Le Havre in 1945/6. It was proposed to order two new train ferries, but owing to war damage there would have been considerable delay in completing the terminal facilities at Le Havre, so the scheme was held in abeyance, never to materialise.

The numerous sidings constructed during 1917/8 for dealing with the traffic for the train ferry and also the barge traffic from the Town Quay. On the left can be seen Western Esplanade with the Old Walls.

Author's collection

Industrial Railways of Southampton

The South of England is not well known for its industrial railways, but Southampton, however, did have its fair share including three separate lines constructed to serve the various wharves on the River Itchen.

Northam Quay Line

As previously recorded under Northam the line to supply the coal for the coke ovens was constructed in 1840. At Northam Quay from about 1855 onwards the firm of Dixon & Cardus Ltd., manufacturers of artificial manure, oil cake and linseed oil, received the raw material for their adjacent mill, and by that time the tramway had been extended to Northam Ironworks – the Engineering & Shipbuilding yard of Day, Summers & Company. It later also served the Northam Steam Sawmills, the property of Messrs. Driver & Company, which were taken over at the end of the First World War by Gabriel Wade & English, and August Pellerin's Le Dansk margarine factory which had been established in 1891 alongside the tramway, west of the timber yard. A siding was also provided near Radcliffe Road to serve the premises of Blokcrete Company Ltd.

Above and below: Northam Quay – A Ruston Hornsby diesel shunter working in 1960 on the line then under control of the Northam Joint Haulage Co., although the locomotive was operated by Pollock, Brown & Co. Ltd. The lower photograph shows the same locomotive working on the diverted line which passed under Northam Road bridge.   *Both E.S. Small*

When the new marshalling yard at Northam was brought into use in 1923 the connection between the Southern Railway and the tramway was made from No.3 siding in the Marshalling yard.

The shipbuilders, Day, Summers & Company went out of business in 1929, and part of their yard was acquired by J.I. Thornycroft & Company Ltd., while the rest was purchased by the scrap metal merchants Pollock, Brown & Company Ltd., (part of Geo. Cohen 600 Group) who were

originally located further down the River Itchen at Union Wharf.

In June 1948, Northam Joint Haulage Ltd. was registered to operate the tramway, the principal shareholders being Auguste Pellerin Ltd., Gabriel, Wade & English Ltd. and George Cohen, Sons & Company Ltd. Dixon & Cardus Ltd. ceased operations during the war and rail traffic for the margarine factory stopped about 1955. The factory was closed on 31st October 1960 having been amalgamated with Mitcham Foods Ltd., a member of the Express Dairy Group.

When the new road bridge over the River Itchen at Northam was constructed in 1953/4 the tramway which until then had continued to cross the Northam Road on the level just west of the Ship Inn was diverted to run nearer the river and passed under the new bridge. The tramway remained open in later years entirely for Pollock Brown's traffic, but the number of wagons involved varied considerably depending on market requirements. In 1984 when British Railways decided to use only air brake wagons, movements over the tramway ceased as the operators did not have a suitable locomotive. The majority of the line can still be seen today, although it has been covered in places.

For many years the tramway was worked by horses, but in January 1904 Dixon & Cardus Ltd. made an application to the Southampton Council for permission to use a small steam locomotive and the first of these was named *Eva*, an 0–4–0ST built by Manning Wardle in 1866. This one was followed by *Nicholson*, an 0–4–2T built by John Fowler in 1907. In 1934 a new four wheeled Muir Hill diesel engine was brought into use, and this locomotive worked the tramway until about 1957, when it was replaced by a Ruston Hornsby 0–4–0 diesel engine provided by Pollock Brown & Company Ltd.

The Chapel Tramway

Shortly after the opening of the Northam Quay Line, another tramway was being constructed to serve the wharves in the Chapel area, including Britannia Wharf, where the firm of E. Pritchard had their Roman cement and lime works. The connection between the LSWR at Chapel and the tramway was made in 1843 when a wagon turntable was installed on a siding adjacent to the running line. The cost of the provision of the turntable was met by Mr. Thomas Bradby, who then owned the tramway. Within a few years various other wharves in the area had been connected to the tramway including Phoenix wharf, Victoria and Sunderland wharves and the Baltic wharf, but the Gas Works were not connected until some thirty years later. The line which crossed Melbourne Street and Marine

Right: Chapel Tramway's 0-4-0ST (Barclay No. 923/1902) crossing Marine Parade with the gas works in the background on 3rd August 1950.   *John A. Bailey*
Below: Chapel Tramway's other 0-4-0ST this one built in 1914 by Peckett (works No. 1375) working on 29th June 1957).
                                                            I.J. Bovey

Chapel Tramway 0-4-0ST locomotive – built by Barclay. At one time this engine carried the name *Lord Fisher* and is now preserved on the East Somerset Railway.   *Bert Moody*

Parade was worked by horses. By 1880 Pritchard's works had been taken over by Hooper & Ashby Ltd. who remained there for many years. The coal firm of J.R. Wood & Company, which was founded in London in 1850 had by about 1882 established a depot at Burnley wharf, which was also served by the Chapel Tramway.

In January 1899 J.R. Wood & Company obtained permission from Southampton Council for a small steam locomotive to operate on the line and the Board of Trade sanctioned the working of the steam engine over the public roadways. During February 1899 J.R. Wood & Company obtained a secondhand locomotive – an 0-4-0ST built by Peckett (Works No.438) in 1884, and during the following month the turntable was replaced with a direct connection giving access to Chapel siding.

The Phoenix Wharf & Coal Company was formed in 1902 and for many years this Company was the principal user of the tramway with many wagons of seaborne coal being forwarded from Phoenix Wharf to various stations throughout Hampshire. The Phoenix Wharf & Coal Company had several of their own coal wagons as did J.R. Wood & Company and also Edwin Jones & Co. Ltd.

J.R. Wood & Company moved up river in 1926 to Belvedere Wharf and the Southampton Gas Light & Coke Company acquired Burnley Wharf, which enabled them to

The same locomotive working along Marine Parade towards Hooper & Ashby's Wharf with wagons of cement in 1964.   *Bert Moody*

enlarge their coke handling facilities. At the end of 1927 the Chapel Tramway Company Ltd. was formed by the users to operate the Tramway. The Phoenix Wharf & Coal Company were then still the principal user, but other firms involved were the Southampton Gas Light & Coke Company, Hooper & Ashby Ltd., Edwin Jones & Company Ltd., the Cement Marketing Company and Dolton, Bournes & Dolton Ltd.

For many years the amount of traffic passing over the Tramway was very considerable, over 100,000 tons each year, and even higher during the Second World War, when supplies of seaborne coal were often delayed. In September 1940 during a heavy air raid the tramway was badly damaged in Marine Parade and was closed for several weeks.

In the early 1950s the outwards coke traffic from the Gas Works amounted to over 20,000 tons each year. Much of this coke went to various fuel merchants at stations in the Hampshire area. Hooper & Ashby Ltd. continued to receive much of their material by rail – in 1953 over 7,000 tons, mainly cement in bags.

As road transport gradually took over the quantity of traffic passing over the Tramway declined and this was hastened by the introduction of the use of surplus gas from Fawley Refinery which in 1957 was being piped from Fawley, thereby reducing the amount of coke being produced. In the 1960s with traffic still on the decline the Tramway became uneconomic to operate, and it was finally closed 31st March 1967.

The original Pecket locomotive was replaced in 1914 by two 0-4-0ST locomotives – a Barclay (Works No.923) built in 1902 and a Peckett (Works No.1375) built in 1914. These were both owned by J.R. Wood & Company and when the Chapel Tramway Company was formed in 1927 they were purchased by the Tramway Company. In 1961 these two locomotives were replaced by another 0-4-0ST built by Barclay in 1915 (Works No.1398) – this locomotive was transferred from the Gas Works at Hilsea and was named *Lord Fisher*, and after closure of the Tramway *Lord Fisher* eventually found a new home on the East Somerset Railway.

Bull's Run Siding

The third siding to serve the Itchen wharves was provided in the 1860s and was connected to the sidings at the south end of Northam yard near Northam Road bridge to give access to Belvidere Works, where the well known local builder Joseph Bull & Sons were located. This firm for many years was involved in the construction of various railway works and buildings in the area. The siding became officially known as Bull's Run – no doubt in view of its early association with the firm. In addition to the line crossing Britannia Road and Belvidere Road there was a secondary line which passed down Britannia Road to the various wharves adjacent to the Yacht Tavern. This portion of the line was subsequently abandoned.

By the turn of the century The Powell Duffryn Steam Coal Company were at Belvidere Wharf and in 1910 made an application for the provision of a second line, and this was provided. During the First World War Belvidere Wharf was taken over by the Government and considerable quantities of coal for the Admiralty was received by rail. Immediately after the war very little use was made of the line for several years. In 1921 the firm Thomas Gater, Bradfield & Company Ltd. acquired Belvidere Wharf and it was their intention to erect a large flour mill on the site

Former BR No. 30096 *Corrall Queen* crossing Britannia Road in June 1964.   *Author's collection*

and for much of the traffic to pass by rail over Bull's Run siding, but this development did not take place, although by 1924 National Benzole Co. Ltd. were using this siding.

In 1926 the coal merchant J.R. Wood & Company moved from Burnley Wharf served by the Chapel Tramway, to Belvidere Wharf. During 1928 a new siding for Dibles (1918) Ltd. was provided to Dibles Wharf off the south line of Bull's Run sidings, the connection being approximately midway between Britannia Road and Belvidere Road.

J.R. Wood & Company acquired in 1926 from the Southern Railway a 0–4–0T No. 0408 *Bretwalda* which had been built for the Southampton Dock Company by Vulcan Foundry Ltd. in 1878. This engine worked the line until scrapped in September 1935 when it was replaced by a Peckett 0–4–0T named *Bristol* which was built in 1923 for the Barnsley Gas Company. In 1940 Southern Wharves Ltd. took over the operation of Dibles Wharf, and in 1952 a new 0–4–0T supplied by Peckett (Works No.2128) was brought into use on the line. In 1963 another former Southampton Docks locomotive – Adams B4 class *Normandy* No.30096 was acquired and this was renamed *Corrall Queen*. In 1968 a diesel engine was acquired and in 1972 *Corrall Queen* was sold to the Bulleid Preservation Society and was transferred eventually to the Bluebell Railway at Sheffield Park and has since been restored to LSWR livery.

In 1967 a large coal concentration depot was developed at Dibles Wharf by Corralls (Powell Duffryn Fuels Ltd.),

thereby enabling various goods yards in the Hampshire area to be closed. Over 90,000 tons of coal and other domestic fuel were dealt with each year. Some of this fuel arrived by sea but a fair proportion of it arrived by train using hopper wagons for quick unloading. With the more recent decline in the use of domestic fuel, Dibles Wharf has been developed for handling various other commodities and in 1987 Corralls moved their fuel depot to Totton Goods yard, and as a result Bull's Run sidings went out of use and the connection to the sidings at the Northam end was removed in 1989.

Electricity Generating Station Siding

In 1896 Southampton Corporation bought out the Southampton Electric Light and Power Company. The original electricity generating station was in the Back of the Walls in Southampton, but in 1902 the Council decided to have a new generating station built on reclaimed land on the western shore near Southampton West station. By December of that year a line had been constructed across the Western Shore Road to the site and this was connected to the down siding near the western end of Southampton Tunnel. At this time No.6 drydock in Southampton Docks was under construction and wagons of filling material from that work passed over the line to enable the land reclamation to be completed. The wagons were drawn across the roadway by horses.

The foundation stone for the new building was laid on the 20th July 1903 and it was decided that the method of traction on the siding would be by electric locomotive taking a supply by means of the overhead trolley system similar to that in use for the tram system. The generating station was brought into use in 1904, but the siding continued to be worked by horses until December 1904, when the overhead system was completed. The siding was inspected by Major J.W. Pringle on 16th December 1904 when the line was passed subject to the speed of movements over the line not exceeding 4 m.p.h., and that a flag man should precede the locomotive or vehicle on each occasion that the public road was crossed.

The first electric locomotive was built on the site. It was constructed mainly from various parts supplied by the Tramway Department, and the total cost of the locomotive was £146 – 8s – 5d. Six wagons were purchased for use at the station and two additional wagons were acquired in order to convey coal from the Chapel Wharves to the station, although some of the coal came direct from the collieries.

By 1930 it was found that the original locomotive was not powerful enough to cope with the number of wagons involved so a new electric locomotive was supplied in 1931 by Baguley (Works No.2048) at the cost of £1139. By the end of the 1930s a daily average of fifty wagons of coal was passing over the siding during the winter months and a third four wheeled locomotive was purchased from Greenwood and Batley (Works No.1620) at the cost of £1595. All three locomotives operated on 550 volts, the same as the Tramway system.

Under nationalisation of the electricity industry the generating station came under the control of the Electricity Generating Board and in 1950 it was decided to use road

Above: Southampton Corporation's electric locomotive No. 2 with a row of wagons for the electricity generating station in the 1930s. *Author's collection*
Below and facing page: The three locomotives which worked the electricity generating station all photographed on 3rd August 1950: *Below:* the original locomotive. The clock tower at Southampton Central can be seen. *Top:* supplied by Baguley in 1931. *Bottom:* supplied by Greenwood & Batley in 1939 at the cost of £1,595. *All by John A. Bailey*

vehicles to bring the coal from Dibles Wharf instead of using the railway, and the siding was taken out of use. The hand point connection was finally removed in April 1964 and that part of the siding in the public roadway was removed in September 1964.

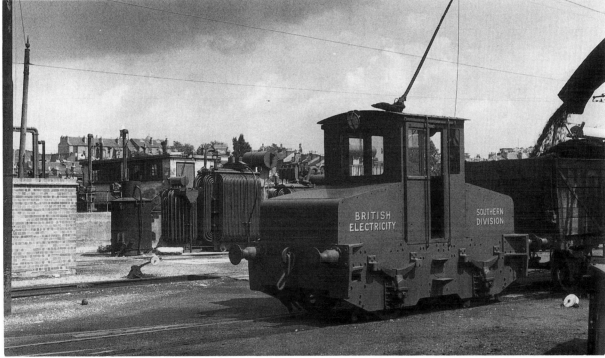

The first locomotive was scrapped about 1953, and the other two locomotives were eventually broken up on the site in March 1960 by the local scrap merchants – Pollock, Brown & Company Ltd. of Northam.

Woolston – Rolling Mills

There was a minor railway which did exist in the Southampton area for a few years during the First World War. This was at the Rolling Mills at Woolston which was built on land, partly owned by the LSWR who had in 1908 acquired a large area of land adjoining the Weston shore for their proposed extension of Southampton Docks.

The railway was standard 4'8½" gauge and served various parts of the Rolling Mills and also the Jetty, but it was completely isolated and not connected to any other railway system.

In some cases cranes were used to move wagons, but at least two steam locomotives are known to have worked there – one was an 0–4–0ST built by Peckett (Works No.596) in 1894 and it is believed to have carried the name Queen Mary, and the other was named Benton, built in 1896 by Black Hawthorn which ended its life at Burt, Boulton & Hayward's yard on the Eling Tramway.

South Western Hotel

The LSWR Act of 1864 allowed the Company to lease land to the Southampton Imperial Hotel Company for the construction of a hotel. The architect for the building was John Norton and construction of the impressive building was carried out during 1865/6.

An application for licence for the sale of intoxicating drinks was first granted in September 1865 on the assurance given by the local representatives that part of the hotel would be opened as from 10th October 1865 as the building was then "in a forward state of completion". The London Directors, however, decided that it was desirable for the whole building to be perfectly completed before opening any part of it. This information was revealed when an application for the renewal of the licence came up before the Licensing Court in September 1866. It was stated in the *Southampton Times* for 1st September 1866 that three months ago the upper part of the building was finished and a contract had been taken for the supply of the furniture.

The opening of the hotel, then known as the Imperial Hotel, was recorded in the *Southampton Times* for 27th July 1867 – "this elegant and imposing structure was opened

South Western Hotel/House – the superb facade on the south side of the building.   *Southern Evening Echo*

A delightful view of the most impressive building still standing in Southampton dockland. The photograph was taken prior to the 1914 war and shows in the foreground the line used by trains passing to and from the Town Quay and the Royal Pier.
Author's collection

When the South Western Hotel was built it was constructed round the ends of the platforms of the LSWR terminus and originally the end of the hotel was open so that the trains could be seen from the roadway. Major alterations were carried out in the 1890s when additional accommodation was provided in the hotel and the openings were fitted with windows. *Southampton Records Office*

for public accommodation last week". One hundred bedrooms were available and it was claimed that the building was the largest of its kind in the provinces. The building had been constructed round the end of the LSWR terminus and on the corner of Terminus Terrace and Canute Road there were several large openings through which the railway could be seen.

Initially the hotel was not a financial success for in May 1868 there was a meeting of the creditors of the Imperial Hotel Company, and in the *Southampton Times* for 17th October 1868 the following announcements appeared – "The Imperial Hotel, this magnificent hotel – built but a year or two since – has been closed for business for some time, and its costly furniture is now in the course of removal to London for sale". During the following week it was announced that the building would be auctioned in November 1868. The *Southampton Times* for 21st May 1870 announced that the hotel had been renamed the South Western Hotel and would shortly be re–opening.

In December 1882 the LSWR purchased the hotel for £18,000 plus £1,177 for wine and other stores, but it was leased until 1899. In 1894 the hotel was thoroughly renovated and refurnished, and it was about this time that the openings on the corner of Terminus Terrace and Canute Road were enclosed and a Visitor's lift ascending to every floor was installed. The proprietor was then a Mr. E.H. Rand – late manager for eight years at Cannon Street Hotel, London. When the lease ended in 1899, the LSWR took over complete control of the building and a contract was placed with Maple & Co. Ltd. for various improvements to be carried out. In the LSWR half yearly report ending December 1900 an amount of £28,000 had been spent of the hotel.

In March 1904 the time ball which until then was located on Gods House near the Town Quay was trans-

ferred to the top of the South Western Hotel and for at least the next thirty years people checked their clocks and watches each day when the ball slid down the pole at 10.00 a.m. Greenwich mean time. The apparatus being operated by an electrical impulse direct from Greenwich.

During the 1920s the hotel was considerably enlarged and three extra storeys were added on the station side and eventually providing a total of about 200 bedrooms. The whole work being completed by the end of 1927. Included in the work was the remodelling of the Terminus station concourse and the provision of the private roadway between the hotel and the station. This roadway remains today and now serves as the main approach to the building.

Without doubt the hey–day of the hotel was between the 1900s and 1930s when many well known people stayed in Southampton on the arrival or departure of the liners. During these years porters in red coats from the hotel met all the principal trains at Southampton West (later Central) station. It was also a social and business centre for the town itself for the majority of the port's principal social functions were held at the South Western.

The hotel ceased to operate as such on 17th August 1940, and it was requisitioned and taken over by the Royal Navy – bearing the name HMS *Shrapnel,* being used for various naval requirements including a transit camp for naval personnel. Various other Government departments used the building after the war and it was finally de–requisitioned in July 1953. Since then it has remained in use for office accommodation for various organisations including the Cunard line and the British Broadcasting Corporation, and was officially renamed South Western House on 1st April 1957.

In May 1985 the building was sold to Shamrock Developments for about £1¾ million and subsequently resold to Percy Bilton (Housing Division).

Railway Steamers

The Outer Dock, the Ocean Village of today, was the home of the railway owned cross channel fleet for nearly sixty years. Here in 1933 are four of the vessels – *Lorina*, *St. Briac*, *Isle of Guernsey* and *Hantonia* or *Normannia* under the large sheer legs which existed near the entrance to the dock for many years. *Associated British Ports courtesy Southampton City Museums*

When the railway first arrived in Southampton several ships were already operating from the Royal Pier to the Channel Islands and to Havre. The two main companies being the New Commercial Steam Packet Company and the South of England Steam Navigation Company.

The directors of the LSWR soon felt that more traffic would be created if they could have some control over these steamers, but in the 1840s the Railway Companies of Britain were not permitted by Parliament to own steamers. In 1842 the Directors appealed to the shareholders of the LSWR to subscribe to help form a South Western Steam Packet Company. There was no great response to this appeal – many considered in those days that shipping was a somewhat risky business financially. The directors, however, pressed on and in 1843 the South Western Steam Packet Company was formed, taking over some of the steamers of the New Commercial Steam Packet Company. The first steamer built for the Company, a paddle steamer of 209 gross tons was appropriately named *South Western* and although built for the Havre service mainly operated to the Channel Islands and St. Malo. In 1845 she was joined by another paddler the *Wonder* which was placed on the Havre service.

In April 1845 the Steam Packet Company obtained the contract to carry mails to and from the Channel Islands. A re-organisation took place in 1846 and a new company

was formed – the New South Western Steam Navigation Company, taking over the assets of the South Western Steam Packet Company and the South of England Steam Navigation Company.

In August 1848 the LSWR were given permission to own and operate steamers, and in the following year the ships of the New South Western Steam Navigation Company were leased by the railway company. This lease expired on the 1st July 1862 and the Railway Company then took over and dissolved the Steam Navigation Company.

Up to 1864 the steamers had embarked and disembarked passengers at the Royal Pier, but in that year arrangements were made for the Docks to be used. At this time as the Docks were not owned by the LSWR the Company developed their own repair yard and workshops at a wharf on the River Itchen and a small drydock was built there and this carried a date stone 'L.&S.W.R. 1877'. In 1902 the repair yard and workshops were closed and the work transferred to the Docks where the LSWR established their own Marine Department workshops. The wharf on the River Itchen was subsequently taken over by James Dredging, Towage & Transport Company Ltd. and the drydock remained in use until a few years ago. This wharf is now privately owned.

The LSWR developed their steamer services to the Channel Islands and to various French ports including St. Malo, Honfleur, Cherbourg and Caen in addition to Havre, and improved vessels were added to the fleet over the years. The paddler *Southampton* entered service in 1860 and lasted until 1898. The last paddler was acquired in 1871 when the Company purchased the *Wolf* from the Burns fleet of Glasgow. She operated mainly on the Cherbourg route and was not withdrawn until 1902. The cargo vessel *Cherbourg*, completed in 1873 gave 57 years service, not being withdrawn until 1930.

Another *South Western* entered service in 1874, being mainly employed on the Southampton – St. Malo route. She lasted for 44 years being finally torpedoed in March 1918. In 1890 a group of three fine ships – *Frederica*, *Lydia* and *Stella* were introduced on the Channel Islands service – they were the first twin screw vessels in the fleet. Four years later saw the introduction of the *Alma* and *Columbia* on the Havre service – these two ships were fitted with separate cabins, the first so equipped in the fleet, until then passengers were accommodated in open type saloons.

In 1905 a pair of cargo vessels – the *Ada* and *Bertha* entered service, and both lasted until the early 1930s. In 1910 the first turbine driven vessels in the LSWR fleet appeared – the *Caesarea* and *Sarnia*, and were placed on the Channel Islands service, while in 1912 two more ships – the *Normannia* and *Hantonia* entered the Havre service, these two were the first cross channel steamers to be fitted with single reduction geared Parsons turbines.

The first Denny built ship to enter the LSWR fleet was the *Lorina* completed in 1918, and after the amalgamation the Southern Railway ordered two more from Denny's the *Dinard* and *St. Briac* which came out in 1924. By then seventeen vessels were attached to the Southampton based fleet, and practically the whole of the Outer Dock (the Ocean Village of today) had been taken over for the railway steamer operations. In 1925 a new Continental Booking Office was constructed to cope with increasing passenger traffic. Part of that building was incorporated into Canute Pavilion in the present Ocean Village development.

Between 1926 and 1928 several new cargo vessels were introduced to cope with increasing cargo traffic, particularly agricultural produce from the Channel Islands and France. In 1929 the very popular *Isle of Guernsey* and *Isle of Jersey* were placed on the Channel Islands service and three years later they were joined by the *Isle of Sark*.

The second world war saw many of these steamers taken up for troop transports or hospital ships and the *Normannia*, *Lorina* and *St. Briac* were lost.

In 1947 a new ship the *Falaise* was completed – mainly for service on the St. Malo route, and in 1952 the *Normannia* entered the Havre service. The passenger services to the Channel Islands were transferred to Weymouth in May 1961, although the cargo service remained at Southampton until September 1972, when it was transferred to Portsmouth. The Havre service was withdrawn in May 1964 and that to St. Malo in September 1964.

Ringwood – one of the railway owned cargo vessels. Built in 1926 the *Ringwood* operated regularly from Southampton until being broken up in 1959 and during that time she carried thousands of tons of produce from the Channel Islands, much of which passed by rail.   *Author's collection*

Postscript

This book was originally published in April 1992, and since that date various developments have taken place, the major one being privatisation resulting in the area coming under the control of South West Trains, a subsidiary of Stagecoach. Other companies are also involved — South Wales & West with the Portsmouth–South Wales services, Virgin Cross Country and Connex South Central with the Bournemouth to Victoria via Gatwick services.

In 1994 Southampton station reverted to its previous name of Southampton Central as some passengers had been alighting at Southampton Parkway for the city. The former goods shed, near Southampton Terminus station, a listed building, has been taken over by Southampton Institute and now forms part of a campus for about 800 students. The site of the former Redbridge Works has been taken over by Associated British Ports and is being used for the storage of imported road vehicles. In 1996 about 800,000 containers passed through Southampton Docks, but the proportion of this traffic now passing by rail has dropped to about 30 per cent. There have been more freight movements into the Docks with trains loaded with export cars arriving about three times each week.

Finally, Southampton International Airport has become very busy and it has been decided to improve the facilities at Southampton Parkway, which serves the Airport, with a new station building to be built on the down side of the line.

A few minor corrections are necessary to the original text. The locomotive depicted in the top photograph on page 18 is a 'C8' and not a 'T9'. Two dates are transposed on pages 36 and 37 — Bevois Street level crossing was closed in January 1964 and Southampton Junction signal box in October 1966. The footbridge at the London end of Southampton Central, referred to on page 74, has been partly renovated and at the time of writing the flags are no longer there. Lastly, there is no longer a connection to the berth in the Western Docks used by P&O as described on page 131.

Bert Moody, May 1997

Bibliography

A History of the Southern Railway *C.F. Dendy Marshall*
The LSWR Vols. I & II *R.A. Williams*
The LSWR in the 20th Century
  J.N. Faulkner and R.A. Williams
A Southern Region Chronology & Record 1803-1965
  R.H. Clark
Old Southampton Shores *J.P.M. Pannell*
The Southampton & Netley Railway *Edwin Course*
Castleman's Corkscrew – The Southampton &
  Dorchester Railway 1844-1848 *J.G. Cox*
History of Southampton 1700-1914 *A. Temple Patterson*
LSWR Locomotives – Adams Classes *D.L. Bradley*
LSWR Locomotives – Drummond Classes *D.L. Bradley*

LSWR Locomotives – Urie Classes *D.L. Bradley*
Locomotives of the LSWR (RCTS) (part 1) *D.L. Bradley*
Making Tracks (at Redbridge) *John Fairman*
Channel Islands Railway Steamers *K. Le Scelleur*
Pullman in Europe *G. Behrend*
Track Layout Diagrams of the SR (Section 2) *G.A. Pryer*
LSWR Appendix to the Working Timetables –
  1911 and 1921
SR Appendix to the Working Timetables – 1934.
Railway Magazines. Southern Daily Echoes and newspapers in Southampton Reference Library. Track Topics – newsletter of Southern Counties Railway Society. South Western Circular – journal of the South Western Circle.

47315 with a well loaded Millbrook to Stratford freightliner service approaching Southampton Tunnel on 17th September 1979.   *I.J. Bovey*